A TASTE OF
ALSACE

A TASTE OF
ALSACE

SUE STYLE

PHOTOGRAPHS BY JOHN MILLER

HEARST BOOKS
NEW YORK

Published in the United States of America in 1991 by William
Morrow and Company Inc., 105 Madison Avenue, New York,
N.Y. 10016.

Published in Great Britain in 1990 by Pavilion Books Limited,
196 Shaftesbury Avenue, London WC2H 8JL, England.

Book design by Lisa Tai.

Library of Congress Cataloging-in-Publication Data

Style, Sue
    A taste of Alsace/Sue Style: photographs by John Miller.
        p.   am.
    ISBN 0-688-10009-4
    1. Style, Sue Cookery, French-Alsatian style. 2. Cookery-
France-Alsace.
    3. Alsace (France)-Social life and customs. I. Title
TX719.2.A4578 1990   90-34664
641.59443'83—dc20   CIP

Printed in Italy

First U.S. Edition
1 2 3 4 5 6 7 8 9 10

AUTHOR'S NOTE
On the umlaut (or lack of) in Gewurztraminer:
as this book deals exclusively with French Gewurztraminers,
from Alsace, the French spelling, which has no umlaut, has been
used.

On the word 'Alsatian':
in order to avoid unfortunate canine connotations, the term
alsacien, both as adjective and noun, has been preferred (with
apologies for apparent affectation).

CONTENTS

INTRODUCTION 9

ASPARAGUS FEVER IN SPRING 22

THE BREADMAKER'S CRAFT 30

FOIE GRAS 38

LIBERTE, EGALITE – ET CHOUCROUTE! 45

THE CHARCUTIER'S ART 54

SNAILS, SYLVANER AND SNAKES 60

THE *FERME AUBERGES* OF
THE HIGH VOSGES 67

THE BUNNERS OF BENNWIHR 75

CHEESE AND WINE IN THE SUNDGAU 81

TOWN *WINSTUBS* AND COUNTRY TAVERNS 88

LES GRANDES TABLES D'ALSACE
L'Auberge de L'Ill 98
Emile Jung 105
The Hussers of Marlenheim 111
Chez Gaertner, Ammerschwihr 118

CO-OPERATIVE EXCELLENCE IN
THE VINEYARDS 126

MADAME FALLER
ET SES FILLES 132

LES GRANDES MAISONS D'ALSACE 140

FROM RASPBERRIES TO HOLLY BERRIES 150

Bibliography 158
Acknowledgements 158
Index 160

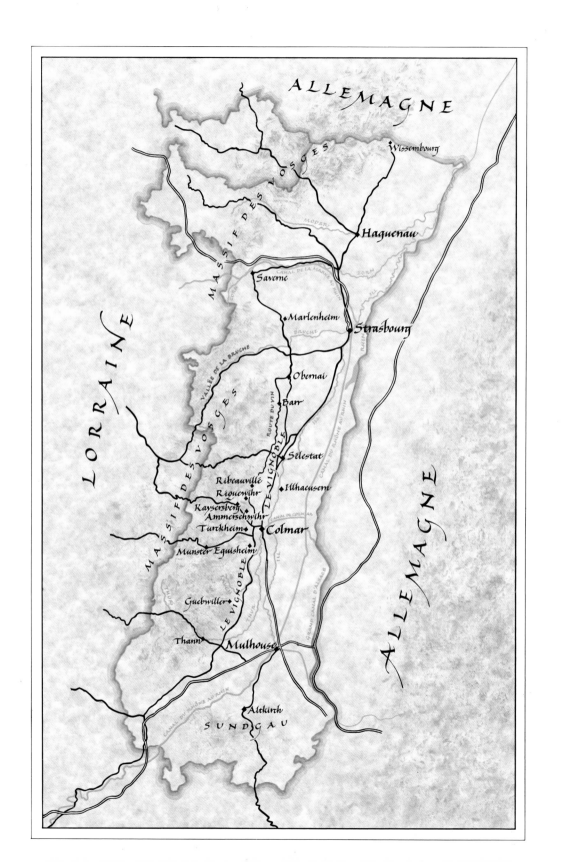

For all those who opened their hearts, homes,
libraries, dining rooms and wine cellars
in order to permit a wider understanding of the
people, places and pleasures of Alsace

Know you the land where the vines and the vineyard
Mingle together with wavering hops?
Know you a place where the elegant foie gras
Is eaten along with peasant pork chops?
Where savoury kraut and tart of the onion
Is heaped on your plate with the quiche of Lorraine?
And you drink and you eat till your belly is bursting
And then in the evening you do it again?

T. A. Layton, Wines and People of Alsace, Cassell, 1970.

INTRODUCTION

Alsace is an interesting place. Beloved by the Swiss, respected (latterly) by the Germans, regarded with some ambivalence by the French of '*l'intérieur*' and known to only a few enlightened Anglo-Saxons, it has always been one of France's best-kept secrets. Embracing two *départements* (the Haut-Rhin and the Bas-Rhin), it stretches in a narrow ribbon from the Swiss border in the south up to the German border some way north of Strasbourg, bounded on one side by the Vosges and on the other by the Rhine. To the west is Lorraine. There is, as André Maurois remarked crisply, 'no Alsace-Lorraine. This is a German creation by Bismarck; there is Alsace, and there is Lorraine.' The name Alsace (*Alesacius*) first appears in mid-seventh century texts and is thought to have developed from either *Ill-sass* (meaning inhabitants of the banks of the Ill) or *Ali-sass* (meaning settlers from elsewhere).

Sheltering in the lee of the Vosges, the province enjoys a semi-continental climate with hot summers and long warm autumns, ideal for market gardeners, wine growers and tourists alike; after Perpignan, Colmar claims to be the sunniest town in France. It is an improbably beautiful place, uncharacteristically (for France at least) neat and tidy, the stuff of which picture postcards are made: medieval towns and villages with higgledy-piggledy, half-timbered houses alight in summer with cascading geraniums and petunias; south-facing slopes neatly contoured with row upon row of vines; richly decorated wrought iron inn signs; great wooden doors from beneath which waft insistent,

9

Half-timbered houses in Colmar

irresistible smells of onion tart, freshly baked bread, new wine, old barrels.

The history of a country has a profound influence in shaping its people, its places and its pleasures. Alsace's history is one of violent swings of the pendulum, from peace to war, from satiety to starvation, from prosperity to poverty, from delight to despair, from Germany to France and back again half a dozen times. Such a confused and chequered past has inevitably produced a complex character. Traditionally the archetypal *alsacien*, satirized in a popular song as *Hans-im-Schnockeloch* ('Johnnie-of-the-mosquitoes'-nest'), is distinguished by his inability to appreciate what he has, coupled with an inconvenient hankering after what he has not. A kinder – and I believe more accurate – description is that of the people of Alsace as *'le carrefour entre le sérieux et la gaieté'*, a sort of crossroads where seriousness and gaiety meet, a nice combination of Germanic thoroughness and reliability with French *joie de vivre*. This duality, nowhere more apparent than in the pleasures of the table, can be traced throughout the history of Alsace.

From celts to romans

Though excavations have shown that Alsace was inhabited during the Stone Age and Bronze Age by wandering hunters, it was not until about 1500 BC that the first settlers – the Celts – began to clear and cultivate the country. In 58 BC the Roman invasion ushered in a long period of prosperity and a burgeoning of culture in many areas, not least in those of food and wine. From this period, claims Irene Kohler in *la cuisine alsacienne*, date a number of delicacies still commonly found in Alsace today: *Kasknepfle*, a gnocchi-like pasta made with curd cheese, evocatively referred to by the Romans as *globi*; *foie gras*; open-faced jam tarts (similar to Linzertorte) criss-crossed by a lattice of spiralled bands of pastry; stuffed breast of veal, all kinds of smoked pork delicacies and a primitive form of pasta. The conquerors brought with them many new vegetables and herbs including cabbages, celery, radishes, cucumbers, parsley, anis and cumin, and fruits of all sorts which were ideally suited to Alsace's hospitable climate: peaches, cherries, plums, apricots and almonds. Though wild vines undoubtedly grew in Alsace before it became part of Gaul, it is generally agreed that the Romans established viticulture as a serious and organised business here. Little wonder that Caesar referred to his newly conquered land as *optimus totius Galliae*, the best of all Gaul.

Alemans, franks and holy roman emperors

With the decline of the Roman Empire came the Alemans, an agricultural people whose language forms the basis of the southern Alsace (Sundgau) dialect today. Few records remain of their way of life or customs, but they are assumed to have adopted many aspects of the lifestyle bequeathed by the Romans, in particular a fondness for oysters, a flair for organised markets and a propensity for building long, straight roads.

Next came the Merovingian period, under the Frankish king Clovis whose spectacular conversion to Christianity in Reims was swiftly followed by a period of intense evangelism. The inevitable increase in demand for communion wine gave a welcome fillip to local wine production, already thriving under the Benedictine monks. They were also engaged in distilling, brewing (using barley or wheat for fermentation), pork salting and smoking and cheese fabrication. The earliest records of Alsace's famous Munster cheese date from this period.

In 750 the deliciously named Pepin the Brief divided the duchy of Alsace into two parts: the Nordgau and the Sundgau, the approximate equivalents of today's two *départements* of the Haut-Rhin and Bas-Rhin. A century later Alsace passed into the hands of Louis the German, apparently for no better reason than that he had expressed a pressing desire to have vines in his kingdom. For the next eight centuries, Alsace's destiny was intimately linked to (and its character indelibly marked by) the Holy Roman Empire – which as more than one history teacher has observed, was neither holy nor Roman, but predominantly German and – at certain moments in its history – distinctly godless.

Under Charlemagne (742-814), the church's power in Alsace increased still further, monasteries and convents flourished and the province prospered. Though the emperor only visited Alsace twice, the inspectors of his provinces came regularly. The impressive list of provisions specified in advance of their visits shows that Alsace in the eighth century was rich both in raw materials and in culinary expertise: butcher's meat, pork, sucking pigs, mutton, lamb, geese, pheasants, hens, eggs, oil, honey, vinegar, cinnamon, pepper, almonds, pistachios, salt, vegetables, fine white bread, cheese, bacon, wine and beer. The orchards of Alsace had developed considerably since Roman times and a list of fruits cultivated during the Carolingian period reads like a horticultural catalogue: pears, apples, plums, chestnuts, wild cherries, hazelnuts, medlars, figs, quince, raspberries, gooseberries, sorb apples, cornel berries and many others.

Louis the Pious (alias the Debonair) is chiefly remembered for his fondness for hunting in the Vosges. Hare, roe deer, red deer and wild boar were commonplace; elk, aurochs, chamois and bear were rare, and reserved for the nobility. He was also fond of fishing for trout in the Thur and further distinguished himself by allowing all wine to travel duty-free, thus giving an early boost to Alsace wine exports. The twelfth and thirteenth centuries were the golden age of Alsace under the Hohenstaufen emperors, one of whom, Frederick I (Barbarossa), claimed Alsace to be 'the dearest of our family possessions'. It was a period of intense urbanization which saw the birth of a powerful merchant class with increasingly sophisticated tastes.

To the late twelfth century belongs the *Hortus Deliciarum*, the work of the noble Abbess of Hohenbourg (Mont Ste. Odile), a unique account of contemporary mores which was tragically lost in the Strasbourg fires of 1870 at the outbreak of the Franco-Prussian war. Traces of the original remain, which show that Alsace's classic *bretzel* was already in existence, and that the noble nuns used knives and forks (but no spoons) at table. It is relatively difficult to find information on the daily diet and general eating habits of the Middle Ages. As Charles Wittmer in his essay *L'Alsace médiévale à table* points

Bed and breakfast in Kaysersberg

11

out, medieval texts were more concerned with the unusual and the unexpected than with the banal and familiar. In spite of this difficulty, he manages to dig out a gem of information on prandial practices in the thermal baths: the lady and gentleman in question would sit facing one another separated by a plank of wood placed across the tub. On this would be served a sustaining meal of carp, or venison, or even bear. Alternatively, there might be fox, mutton or sausages with turnips, with pears poached in red wine for dessert.

Meanwhile, the daily fare of less exalted folk – such as the masons working on the Saint Léger church in Guebwiller in 1182 – consisted of unlimited garlic and bread; on Sundays, however, they could feast to their hearts' content on meat (probably pork) and 'all manner of good things'. Practically anything that moved was hunted down mercilessly; even the poor titmouse (*Meise*) was on sale in the markets. On the frequent days of abstinence decreed by the church calendar, eggs alternated with pancakes (*Eierkuchen*), mushrooms, wild greens and fish, particularly salt herrings which were shipped up the Rhine from Holland.

A century later in 1264 we find records of the establishment of the corporation of bakers in Strasbourg (the oldest in Alsace), which suggests that the profession was already quite highly developed. Later the pastry cooks formed their own separate corporation, an important branch of which was that of the *Lebküchler* or gingerbread bakers. The *Lebkuchen* (or *pains d'épices*) were sweetened with honey and spiced initially only with ginger. With the crusades the range of spices increased and became more and more exotic, as did the beautiful moulds for making them. They are still an essential feature of any Alsace fair or market.

The thriving monasteries and bishoprics (notably those of Strasbourg and of Basle) continued to furnish wine for both religious and secular purposes, for local consumption and for export. Contemporary accounts

A rich array of breads

show that important markets for the wines of 'Aussey' or 'Ossey' (as they were then known) were Scandinavia, Holland, England, Spain, Germany, Switzerland and (from 1220, when the Gotthard Pass was opened) Italy. Many of these are still faithful importers today. By the end of the fourteenth century, claims Guy Renvoisé in his *Guide des vins d'Alsace*, 'the objective of wine-growing Alsace was one of quality.' Then the picture changed dramatically. A succession of bad winters followed hard on the heels of poor harvests and then the crowning disaster of bubonic plague. For this the Jews proved a convenient scapegoat, and they were viciously persecuted in the pogroms of 1336 and 1349. Though the Hundred Years War did not directly involve Alsace, wandering mercenaries pillaged and ransacked the countryside and commandeered all available foodstuffs.

RENAISSANCE, REFORMATION AND COUNTER-REFORMATION

The Renaissance in the Rhine lands brought (apart from the Gütenberg bible and Grünewald's incomparable

Issenheim altarpiece) a welcome return to peace and prosperity. Excess and riotous living became the order of the day, a fact which drew the fire of both religious and secular writers and orators. The Reformation brought with it a noted killjoy named Sebastien Brant, who in his satirical work *der Narrenschiff* bitterly attacked the people's excessive preoccupation with 'filling the belly like a cow's stomach and drinking to the health of all and sundry' which can lead 'only to losses and lawsuits'. It was an attitude shared by his contemporary Geiler of Kaysersberg: 'Your faith is in eating and drinking,' he thundered from his mid-sixteenth century Strasbourg pulpit, 'in bottles, gambling and cards!' Things reached such a pitch that laws (*Polizeiordnungen*) were introduced restricting not only the quantity and nature of the food to be served at functions such as weddings and receptions, but the number of guests and the duration of the feast. Jean Fischart of Strasbourg, who in 1575 made a rather liberal translation into German of Rabelais' Gargantua and detailed over fifty pretexts for a party, presumably thought little of such ordinances.

A spectacular feast (the description of which has doubtless been richly embellished over the centuries) was that of the legendary Martin Kulm, a soldier home on leave in 1520 who booked himself into an inn in Thann. Claiming that he would be joined at table by a band of friends, he rolled up his sleeves and proceeded to tuck into a meal of bread soup, two pounds of boiled beef, a dish of *choucroute* garnished with a crusty piece of pork, a veal roast, a chicken fricassee, three pigeons, ten thrushes, a plate of trout from the nearby River Thur and five jugs of Rangen wine with which to wash it all down. History does not relate what happened to his friends; all we know is that he demolished the meal unaided, rose from the table, belched several times and set off into the night.

A noted visitor to the area in 1580 was Montaigne. In his essays he commented approvingly on the beautiful fish cookery of the Alsace cooks and on the fact that people did not water down their wine. He also remarked that they seemed more concerned with their meals than with the decoration of their houses – which simply shows that the *alsaciens* have always had a right and proper sense of priorities.

The sixteenth century marked the beginning of a rich fund of gastronomic literature. In 1507 Anne Keller, the wife of a Doctor Wecker in Colmar wrote a book which combined (as was common in those days) both recipes and dietary information, and was based on the Hippocratic theory of the four humours. It is divided into four parts; vegetables, fruits, beasts of the earth (meat and game) and beasts of the water (fish, snails and frogs), the idea being that food is matched to mood. An infusion of almonds in milk seems to be a sort of universal panacea, and there are recipes involving *Schnitzen*, the dried apples and pears still extensively used today in both desserts and meat dishes throughout the Rhine valley.

Fifteen-thirty-nine saw the first edition of Jérome Bock's *Kräuterbuch*, so successful that it was reprinted three times (a copy of the 1551 edition can be seen today in the University Library in Strasbourg). Principally a herbal, it also includes recipes and details of conserves (strawberry) and pickles (cabbage) to be put up during the year. He takes a dim view of blackberries ('such berries are food for the poor who have only modest means') but enjoys mushrooms cooked with the ubiquitous *Schnitzen* and spiced up with ginger, basil and mint. He claims, with understandable smugness, that while 'we may not have nutmeg or cloves like other people, we do have the exceptional saffron.' Spices, though, were still the preserve of the rich; most contented themselves with wild herbs of which rosemary, thyme, hyssop, sage and burnet are only a small selection. Pork is frequently mentioned, especially in the company of cabbage. A sucking pig is recommended for Sunday, 'carrying in his mouth an apple, symbol of civil rights [the pig's?] and domestic ties attaching him to the family and to society.' New vegetables include artichokes, asparagus (probably wild), spinach and peas; sweetcorn, sugar, tomatoes and turkey all make their entrance from the New World; potatoes are commented on as a curiosity rather than as food. It took until the beginning of the nineteenth century for them to become an integral part of the Alsace diet. Cereals were the staples, in the form of thick, soup-like purées (muss) and made variously of millet, white beans, barley, rice, peas or wheat.

The climax came in 1671 with the publication of the book which has been acclaimed by Messrs. Drischel, Poulain and Truchelut in l'Histoire et recettes de l'Alsace Gourmande as 'the birth certificate of Alsace gastronomy': the Abbot Buchinger's Kochbuch (also in the Strasbourg University Library). Though subtitled 'for the use of religious and lay households', it was aimed principally at Benedictine and Cistercian monasteries and gives recipes and suggested menus for different occasions and seasons.

The good Abbot has little time for lentils ('they are no use; only for the servants, or for soup, or cooked like peas, with onions'), but strongly recommends lard for the preparation of both meat and vegetables, except on days of abstinence. Three recipes are given for beavers' tails and trotters, suitable for fast days since the flesh of this river-dweller was not counted as meat; pâté and terrine recipes are legion, containing anything from peacock to squirrel to monkfish livers. A sage, marjoram, rosemary and orange and lemon zest marinade is recommended for goat to be roasted on the spit; cows' udders seem to have held a particular gastronomic appeal; uneviscerated snipe is to be cooked with spiced bread underneath to catch the juices. François Voegeling wonders idly in La Gastronomie Alsacienne whether we would nowadays relish Buchinger's dish of boiled beef snout stuck with cinnamon and cloves, dried on a rack

and served with a sweet sauce of breadcrumbs or flour, wine, currants, almonds, ginger, pepper and cinnamon. Noodles appear for the first time, along with mention of another pasta, Wasserstriwela (nowadays known as Spätzle) which actually goes back to Roman times. There are helpful hints on how to make ink – and how to remove stains. With its judicious combination of intriguing recipes, social commentary and sound common sense, it is the most complete of the early Alsace gastronomical works and the one most extensively quoted from.

FROM GERMANIC IMPERIALISM TO FRENCH MONARCHY

The eight formative centuries of Germanic influence in Alsace were drawing to a close as the Holy Roman Empire disintegrated into the tragedy of the Thirty Years War (1618-48). The Protestant Swedes, provoked by the French to go to the aid of the German Princes, were pitted against the Catholics headed by the house of Hapsburg. Alsace – not for the first, nor for the last time in its history – was the principal battleground, the country was laid bare, its population decimated, its vineyards reduced to charred stumps, its survivors condemned to a diet of acorns, goatskins, grass, even human flesh. At the conclusion, under the terms of the peace Treaty of Westphalia (1648), the Hapsburgs handed over to France all previously held rights to the province. Seduced, no doubt, by the promise of religious tolerance guaranteed under the Edict of Nantes, Alsace for the first time in its history became French. The region was largely repopulated by settlers from Switzerland, the Black Forest, Austria, Lorraine and other parts of France, each of whom added their own gastronomic traditions to the melting pot which was Alsace in the seventeenth century.

By 1681 Louis XIV was looking over the Vosges from Versailles and exclaiming over his new territory: 'Quel

Early morning mists in the Vosges

beau jardin!'. Without any pressure from Paris ('the affairs of Alsace must not be interfered with'), the province of its own volition became increasingly French in spirit, proud to belong to the country generally regarded as the most civilized in Europe at the time, yet always retaining its Germanic customs, characteristics and dialects. By 1744, when Louis XV visited Strasbourg, the people were clearly more than ready to fête their French king. At a banquet laid on in his honour there is a nice description of members of the Butchers' Corporation, presumably bursting with pride, carrying in on their shoulders a whole ox stuffed with two sheep and a hundred pounds of sausages, surrounded by six sucking pigs, twelve geese, twelve ducks and thirty-six capons. It was an auspicious period and one of intense industrial and agricultural growth.

At least one visitor, however, a certain disgruntled Doctor Maugue, thought little of the food he was offered, and wrote in 1706 that it was 'about as good as you could expect, given the area in which it is grown. By its nature it is coarse and glutinous – spinach, root vegetables, turnips (raw and cooked), beans, peas, rice, dried fruits, pearl barley and cabbage, cabbage everywhere . . . Their soups consist of a couple of pounds of beef which have wallowed around in a huge pan of boiling water, without any redeeming benefits of herbs or spices.' Maybe if he'd been lucky enough to be served his soup from one of the superb faïence tureens made soon afterwards by the Hannong family in Strasbourg (now in the Musée du Château des Rohan), he might have been prepared to overlook its contents. Certainly if he had lingered long enough to sample Jean-Pierre Clause's *pâté de foie gras de Strasbourg*, created in 1762, in which for the first time *foie gras* was wrapped in a farce and encased in pastry, he could not have failed to be impressed.

FROM FRENCH REVOLUTION TO PRUSSIAN OCCUPATION

A feather in Alsace's patriotic cap was the fact that the French national anthem, initially entitled the Battle Hymn for the Army of the Rhine, later *La Marseillaise*, was composed in Strasbourg by a certain Rouget de l'Isle in 1792. The excesses of the Revolution shocked the traditionally tolerant *alsaciens*, though they embraced some of the new ideas which it brought. Practically speaking, although the breaking up of the huge wine-growing estates (previously in church or private hands) looked temptingly egalitarian, the subsequent fragmentation of the vineyards was definitely detrimental to Alsace's wine trade. The establishment of the Empire brought with it a veritable Napoleonic cult; possibly the *alsaciens* were readily able to identify with this outsider from another far-flung French province, and to admire his power and ruthlessness. It was something of a mutual admiration society: Napoleon expressed a special affection for his Alsace regiments, attached as ever to their dialect: 'Let them speak their jargon,' he said indulgently, 'for they fight like true French swordsmen.'

In 1825 Brillat-Savarin published his *Physiologie du Goût* in which the *alsaciens* were gratified to learn that among his *éprouvettes gastronomiques* were listed three of the region's classic dishes: a plate of *choucroute* all set about with sausages and crowned with Strasbourg bacon, the inevitable *pâté de foie gras de Strasbourg* in the form of a fortress; and a huge carp from the Rhine.

Between 1829 and 1833 (at about the time that Eliza Acton's *Modern Cookery* appeared in England) Marguerite Spoerlin's *Oberrheinisches Kochbuch*, later translated as *La cuisinière du Haut-Rhin*, was published. It was the first Alsace cookbook to be directed specifically at '*les jeunes ménagères et aux mères de famille*' (young wives and mothers). In the familiar preamble about how this book differs from any others hitherto published, she invokes the great simplicity and strict economy of her recipes, which nonetheless conserve all the flavour and good taste which is the essence of good cooking. It is full of sound advice, as valid today as it was then: 'avoid serving foods which are out of season' and 'do not be tempted to think that expensive foods are necessarily the best'. Her recipes for *soupe aux escargots* and her *asperges en mermelade* sound as fresh and modern today as they

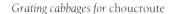

Grating cabbages for choucroute

must have in the mid-nineteenth century. It is tempting to wonder whether Isabella Beeton, whose *Household Management* of 1861 was similarly directed at young housewives, and who spoke good French, was familiar with Marguerite Spoerlin's work.

The lawyer Charles Gerard's *L'Ancienne Alsace à table*, published in 1862 (and reissued in a limited edition in 1971 with an excellent preface by the Haeberlin brothers) was not a cookbook but a masterly study of the eating and drinking habits of Alsace through the ages. Though there are inaccuracies (such as the information on the origins of *choucroute*, and on Clause's *pâté de foie gras*), it is nonetheless an interesting, exhaustive study. He concludes that there is 'certainly no place where the need for conviviality is more energetically demonstrated than in Alsace, nor where it is more amply satisfied'.

In 1870, the German (Prussian) armies under Bismarck marched west and proclaimed Alsace a *Reichsland*. From this period date the famous satirical drawings of Hansi (they make poignant contemporary postcards), depicting Alsace under the Prussian yoke and exhorting the people never to forget that they were French. Thousands emigrated, many to America; Bartholdi, in exile in Paris, created his famous Statue of Liberty, saying that it represented for him precisely that freedom which he and his fellow *alsaciens* were currently denied. *Choucroute*, hitherto the Alsace dish *par excellence*, vanished from the tables of Strasbourg and Colmar, while in Paris at the Brasserie Lipp which opened in 1872, it became something of a *plat de résistance*. A group of artists, sculptors and musicians, united under the aegis of Auguste Michel (a noted epicure and *fabricant de foie gras*) chose to express their resistance through a series of spectacular – and studiously French – meals. The beautifully illustrated menus of this select dining club, known as the *Kunschthafe* (*Kunscht* meaning 'art', and *Hafe* cooking pot) can be seen in the Strasbourg University Library.

French patriotism fostered from the cradle

The occupation years signalled disaster for the vineyards, as Alsace wines were ignominiously used as bulk blending material for German wines. Bugs, beasts, bad harvests and disease all took their toll, the phylloxera aphis munched its way steadily through the vineyards of France and in 1876 began to deal its devastating blow to Alsace. Many growers gave up the unequal struggle at this time and sold their land or allowed it to revert to scrub. The agricultural picture in the nineteenth century was more positive, with wheat, sugar beet, hops, potatoes and tobacco all flourishing. The arrival of a certain pastor Heyler in northern Alsace in 1873, who brought with him the secrets of asparagus culture was a bright spot in the gastronomic landscape.

Escoffier in his 1902 *Guide Culinaire* seems (like France at the time) to have rather lost Alsace from view, making only a perfunctory allusion to *choucroute*, turnips, bacon and noodles – as if that were all Alsace had to offer. Sadly, it must be said this limited view of traditional *alsacien* cooking is still fairly commonly held by many French of '*l'intérieur*'.

THE TWO WORLD WARS

The occupation fused inexorably with the First World War, after which – in the colourful words of the authors of *L'Histoire des Alsaciens* – 'the lost province threw itself at the feet of the mother country.' Alsace still considered itself to be French, even if others had forgotten. Strenuous attempts were made in the vineyards to improve growing stock by grafting disease-resistant plants onto existing vines; hybrids were outlawed; the proportion of 'noble' to 'common' vines began to come under the microscope; yields were reduced and plantings in the plain were discouraged. At last Alsace looked like regaining its fourteenth-century renown as an area of quality wines.

In September 1939 when Hitler invaded Poland, approximately one third of the population of Alsace was summarily evacuated to the other side of France; in 1940 Alsace was once more occupied by the Germans. ('Alsace is like a lavatory – permanently occupied', commented Tomi Ungerer, one of the province's more controversial and colourful sons recently.) Berets were forbidden – 'They soften the brain', remarked a certain Gauleiter Wagner – and high German was declared the only permissible language. One hundred and forty thousand men between the ages of seventeen and thirty-eight were conscripted into the German army or navy (some even into the SS), forced to fight on opposite sides from their own flesh and blood. Refusal to comply meant certain death, or torture for the family members left behind. About forty-three thousand of them never returned. They were called the *malgré-nous* ('against our will'). Jacques-Louis Delpal in his excellent guide to Alsace comments that forty-five years later, these people continue to be 'ulcerated by the inability of the French of *'l'intérieur'* to understand the drama of their compulsory military service'.

The last months of 1944 were peculiarly painful ones for the vineyard villages, as the war drew convulsively to a close. People took refuge in the cellars which were stocked only with wine, apples and potatoes. Worse than hunger was the lack of drinking water, for the wells were outside. *Schnapps* was used as fuel, for fear that the smoke from fires would make them a target. Mouldy pumpernickel discarded by the German soldiers, meat from the odd cow caught in crossfire, a few eggs gleaned from the ruins, or some goats' milk from a wandering beast – these constituted the diet of the people of Bennwihr in December 1944.

In 1945 the painstaking restoration of towns and villages began, the vineyards were cleared of mines and replanted, and many co-operatives formed. The fields and orchards were once more cultivated. Alsace was back on the road to becoming the wine cellar, granary and well-stocked larder of the Middle Ages.

THE FOOD OF ALSACE TODAY

Tradition has it that a traveller passing through Alsace was once asked whether he preferred to eat in France or Germany. 'In Germany', he replied, 'there's plenty of it, but it's bad; in France it's good, but there's not enough; in Alsace, there's plenty and it's good!' French flair coupled with German quantity, the best of all possible worlds. The Alsace dialect is liberally larded with sayings which bear witness to the important role played by food and drink. *'Esse un trinke halt Lib un Seel zamme'* suggests that 'eating and drinking hold body and soul together', while *'Asse un nit getrunke isch so viel as gehunke'* can be loosely translated as 'eating without a drink is like walking with a limp'. François Voegeling in *La Gastronomie Alsacienne* observes drily that 'the quality of the Alsace appetite is situated somewhat above the national average'.

Unlike in some countries (particularly Anglo-Saxon ones), in Alsace the distinction between 'restaurant food' and 'home cooking' is extremely blurred. Many of the traditional family dishes (*choucroute, Baeckeoffe*, boiled beef with salads, onion tart, *matelote*, to name but a few) are as likely to be found in a tavern in tourist Riquewihr as on the table of the Hugel family (though it is probably fair to say that Madame Hugel's version will be better). The Club Prosper Montagné does a great job keeping alive many old recipes by annually awarding a prize to the housewife who comes up with the best version of a traditional Alsace speciality. Recent prize-winning recipes included *tourte de la Vallée de Munster*, onion tart, *tarte au fromage blanc*, *kugelhopf* and *pot-au-feu à l'alsacienne*.

The tradition of eating out is also well established. It may be simply Sunday lunch, or it may be a baptism, a first communion, a special birthday or anniversary. Maybe it's just for fun, a good meal and a welcome break for the cook. It is not surprising, therefore, to find that Alsace is one of those delicious regions of France which is so well-endowed with wonderful restaurants that the stars cannot all be squeezed into the map at the front of the Michelin guide and a special box has to be appended. Not only does it boast some extremely talented chefs, but also – thanks to the richness and variety of the ancient gastronomic culture outlined above – it provides them with an unparalleled supply of regional ideas and influences on which to draw for inspiration.

For the interested visitor, one of the best things about eating out in the area is that however *haute* the *cuisine*, little echoes of Alsace will always remain: hop shoots with lightly poached eggs (Emile Jung, Le Crocodile, Strasbourg); a mini-*Baeckeoffe* perfumed with truffles which has come a long way from its humble washday origins to grace the tables of the Auberge de l'Ill; little cubes of brawn (head cheese) sitting on a mound of lentils and lamb's lettuce and flavoured with a warm horseradish dressing (Robert and Michel Husser, Le Cerf, Marlenheim) or *Schniederspättle*, the region's ravioli, accompanied by frogs' legs in a chervil sauce (Antoine Westermann, Buerehiesel, Strasbourg). The '*beau jardin*'

The village of Riquewihr

over which the Sun King sighed is a garden which continues to furnish its chefs with food for thought.

Spectacular though these starred establishments undoubtedly are, it would be a pity (not to mention damaging to wallet and to waistline) to concentrate too much on the *grandes tables*. In spring, people feast with impressive zeal on plainly boiled asparagus with hollandaise, mayonnaise and vinaigrette. In summer a day's walk up in the cool of the Vosges may culminate in lunch at a *ferme auberge*, featuring a flaky-crusted pork pie, boiled ham with potatoes, a fruit tart furnished from the hedgerows and home-grown Munster cheese, all served simply and without ceremony in the farm house or yard.

Autumn is the time for *flammekueche*, Alsace's answer to pizza, a fragile rectangle of thinly stretched bread dough spread with curd cheese, bacon and onions and baked till bubbling and golden in a special oven. In winter, the *Winstubs* of Strasbourg are tightly packed with people tucking into every conceivable part of the pig; smoked, salted, spiced or sauced, and served hot or

Sizzling tartes à l'oignon

Gérard commented in the 1860's, 'in Alsace, the institution of the pâté has always rested on broad and reassuring foundations'. *Plus ça change* . . .

From the baker you could choose a different sort of loaf each day for a fortnight and never repeat yourself, for Alsace draws on its German, Austrian, Swiss, Jewish, and French connections to produce a seemingly inexhaustible range of loaves and rolls of differing shapes and sizes. The baker may also be a pastry chef, in which case the temptations of a slice of rhubarb, apricot, mirabelle or bilberry tart may prove altogether too much – if a slab of cheesecake with kirsh-soaked raisins or a sampling of pear charlotte redolent with locally distilled *eau de vie de poire* William doesn't catch your eye first.

The choice of cheese is simplified by the fact that Alsace has only one native offering: Munster, trenchantly described by local author Jean Egen as 'powerfully dialectic, marrying pleasure with repulsion, delight with pestilence . . . German smell, French flavour, a typically *alsacien* cheese'. Take care, therefore, to pack it in an airtight container, especially if you are planning to cross any borders: winding down the window to declare your merchandise becomes a hazardous business (for customs officers).

Finally, for a different sort of outdoor feast, try any of the numerous *fêtes* held throughout the summer and autumn, each one dedicated to a particular speciality; bread, *kugelhopf*, snails, cheesecake, cherries, fruit of all sorts, *tourtes*, *tartes*, *choucroute* – and wine.

WINES, BEER AND EAUX DE VIE

In its wines as in its food, Alsace borrows from both its French and its German past to produce something which is uniquely *alsacien*. A current campaign by the Comité Interprofessional du Vin d'Alsace, the region's official wine body, refers to them as 'The French Exception'. The problem is that because many of the grape varieties sound German, (and perhaps also because some people

cold with *choucroute* and salads. Alternatively on the *Route du Vin* in the *caveaux* run by the local wine-grower or co-operative, onion tart may be the order of the day, or – by special request from a party of hungry walkers – *Baeckeoffe*, a robust one-pot meal which was traditionally a Monday morning washday dish, entrusted to the care of the baker's oven while Madame got on with the laundry. The *patron* emerges through the swing doors with a flourish, resting the immense decorated pottery dish on his ample stomach. Setting it down in the middle of the table, he carefully prises away the sealing band of dough, the diners incline in eager anticipation, off comes the lid and in one moment all the flavours and fragrances of Alsace are released: pork, lamb, beef, pigs' trotters and herbs, all layered with slices of firm, waxy potatoes and marinated overnight in Riesling.

When it comes to provisions for the picnic basket, decision-making skills and an element of self-control are both crucial. The final selection between the different pâtés, terrines, hams, pies, quiches and tarts on offer in the best butchers' shops is no easy task. As Charles

still have a rather vague idea of Alsace's geography) the wines of Alsace are all too often confused with inferior, low-alcohol, sugared beverages from the other side of the Rhine. This is unflattering and inaccurate, for Alsace wines nowadays are almost invariably well made, full-bodied, aromatic and – above all – dry. Robert Parker describes them as 'among the greatest white wines of France', yet 'terribly and curiously undervalued, and to a large part misunderstood by the wine-drinking public'; Hugh Johnson claims that 'Alsace guarantees a certain quality and a certain style more surely than any other wine region. It makes brilliantly appetizing, clean-cut and aromatic wine to go with food, and at a reasonable price.' Though many of us will rue the day when the price reflects the quality, it is certainly time Alsace wines were better understood.

Alsace wines differ from other French wines for many reasons, not least because they are conveniently and simply classified by grape variety: Riesling, Alsace's king of wines; Gewurztraminer, heady and intensely aromatic; Pinot Gris, rich and opulent; Muscat, pure grapes in the glass with an unexpectedly dry finish; the zesty, fresh Pinot Blanc and Sylvaner; and Pinot Noir, often made as a light red or rosé. Edelzwicker is not a grape but the only blended wine in the area, where the balance of grape varieties included is decided by the grower, giving some interesting local variations. Crémant d'Alsace, the region's champagne method sparkling wine (white or rosé), provides festive bubbles and makes an excellent *Kir royale*. Try it also with *crème de mûre* (blackberry), *myrtille* (bilberry), or *pêche* (peach), all of them made locally.

Though Alsace is very much a land of the grape, hops are still a distinctive part of the northern Alsace landscape and delicious beers are brewed. Last but far from least are the *eaux de vie*, clear spirits distilled from fruits and berries found in the orchards, vineyards and hedgerows of the plains, and the hillsides and forests of the Vosges. Served after many a memorable meal they make a fitting conclusion to the proceedings.

An area which has been bitterly and bloodily fought over, shaped by the Romans and the Holy Roman Empire, scarred by the Thirty Years War, smiled on by the Sun King, tossed back and forth between two great European nations, Alsace is now definitely part of France – yet somehow not altogether French; definitely not German – yet somehow Germanic. I hope that through the people, places and pleasures met in this book, you will catch glimpses of what makes it such a uniquely fascinating and rewarding place to visit.

Basle, Switzerland
August 1989

Vineyards basking in autumn sunshine

ASPARAGUS FEVER IN SPRING

No one is admitted to the Asparagus Fraternity who is not cheerful, fond of asparagus, an expert in fine wines, a gallant gentleman or an admirer of the male sex.
ARTICLE 1 OF THE CHARTER OF THE *CONFRÉRIE DES ASPERGES.*

It is difficult to convey to anyone who has never been to Alsace in the spring the quasi-religious fervour inspired by the great god asparagus. At Anglo-Saxon tables this vegetable, guiltily classified as a luxury item, might make a furtive appearance once or twice a year, probably eked out with irrelevant accompaniments like pastry or eggs. In Alsace, on the other hand, there are restaurants in the asparagus-growing areas which base their entire reputation and *raison d'être* on the vegetable. They are open only from mid-April until St John's Day (June 24th), serve only asparagus feasts, and cater for

An asparagus festival in Village Neuf

added incentive to consumption. Probably most important of all in an area which can suffer long and rigorous winters are the attendant implications of the arrival of spring. Michel Kauffman, in his *Eloge de l'Asperge* (Ode to Asparagus), speaks of 'this miracle which is annually renewed' and refers to asparagus as the harbinger of fine days, its spring beauty giving us hope for the months to come.

Consumption of asparagus in Alsace has a long and well-chronicled history. Records at the Roman settlement of Augst just up the Rhine show that the plant was already under cultivation in the sandy soils beside the river. There are drawings of wild asparagus in Jérome Bock's sixteenth century herbal (*Kräuterbuch*), and a recipe suggesting its use in salads. The fact that the latter

Insignia of a member of the Confrérie des Asperges

whole families or groups of friends, who will certainly make several such pilgrimages during the short season. Huge trestle tables and long wooden benches are the order of the day, napkins are tucked into collars beneath expectant faces, and the serious business gets underway: 1 kilo (2 lb) per person has been known to disappear without apparent difficulty. The mighty white spears are served naked and unadorned save for the regulation three sauces (vinaigrette, mayonnaise, hollandaise) and thick slices of smoked, raw and cured ham.

Such fervour is not easily explained, particularly to Anglo-Saxons. Perhaps after the stodgy stews and starchy vegetables of the winter months, the body craves the slight astringency of asparagus with its sharp accompanying sauces. The fact that it is rich in vitamins, and is an excellent diuretic (hence its irreverent Edwardian sobriquet, Housemaid's Delight), may be an

Asparagus peeling at La Charrue, Hoerdt

were dressed with oil – an unheard-of luxury for any but the most affluent households – suggests that the delicacy would have been confined to a tiny fraction of the population. Buchinger, a century later, gives six recipes in his *Kochbuch*. Marguerite Spoerlin's nineteenth-century *Cuisinière du Haut-Rhin* gives an intriguing-sounding recipe for *asperges en marmelade*: only the tips are used, lightly cooked and served with a 'butter sauce' which on closer inspection turns out to be a hollandaise. By the early 1900s, asparagus begins to figure regularly on wedding menus – always a good barometer of gastronomic trends.

It was in the late nineteenth century, however, that asparagus really began to be a force to be reckoned with in Alsace. A pastor named Heyler arrived from Algeria to take up the parish of Hoerdt in northern Alsace, where living standards at the time bore little resemblance to those of today. Searching for a solution which would enable his impoverished flock to make best use of the limited resources available to them, he found that the apparently unpromising, sandy soil of the region was ideal for growing asparagus culture. In 1873 the industry was born.

White asparagus is king in Alsace; green is regarded as a mere commoner. For years I fondly imagined that they were two quite different plants. After a visit to the market gardens in Village-Neuf with Monsieur Girroy, president of the market gardeners of the Haut-Rhin, I realized the error of my ways; white asparagus would

also be green if it were only allowed to frolic above ground. Instead it is blanched by means of trenching, and cut at crack of dawn each day before any tips have a chance to emerge and take colour. The quality of the soil is crucial in the growing of white asparagus, since the entire plant is interred in it. Some even go so far as to suggest that different soils give different flavours. Perhaps one day there will be asparagus *grands crus* . . .

Heyler's parish in the Bas-Rhin is still the most significant production area in Alsace, while in the Haut-Rhin most of the asparagus is grown beside the Rhine around Village-Neuf – conveniently close to the border with Switzerland, where asparagus appetites are insatiable, and the purchasing power of the Swiss franc unquestionable. It is also, appropriately, the home of Monsieur André Weber, *le Grand Aspergier d'Alsace*, founder of the *Confrérie des Asperges* and indefatigable champion of the asparagus cause.

One May evening we decided to join the fray. The booking was made, the pilgrimage undertaken in good faith. The only snag was that approximately 247 other people had all had the same idea on exactly the same evening, at the same restaurant and at the same time. The problem seemed to stem from the fact that the ever-obliging owners, acutely conscious of the brevity of the season, hadn't found it in their hearts to say no to *any* of us. Frantic consultations ensued, while desperate glances were cast at row upon row of firmly ensconced customers. Would we mind waiting for a second sitting? Of course we wouldn't. We stood in serried ranks in the car park, cheerfully quaffing Edelzwicker plied through the kitchen window. We caught candlelit glimpses of pink-faced pilgrims tucking into their asparagus in the inner sanctum, and consoled ourselves with the thought that in due course all sorts of interesting things come to those who wait. We waited, and they did.

Evening-picked asparagus

Petites Mousses aux Asperges

*Palest green spear-topped mousses, lightly set with gelatine,
turned out and served with salad*

Makes 8
500 g/1 lb green asparagus
6 sheets gelatine, soaked in cold water
until floppy
or 1 tbsp unflavoured gelatine powder
sprinkled onto 3 tbsp water
salt and pepper
250 ml/9 fl oz/1 cup whipping cream
a small amount of dressed salad (e.g. lamb's
lettuce/corn salad, cress, oakleaf etc.)

Oil lightly 8 ramekins (125 ml/4½ fl oz/½ cup size).
Trim the asparagus and cook it in boiling salted water
for 20 minutes until quite tender. Drain asparagus,
reserving 1 cup cooking water. Put this in a small pan
and dissolve the soaked gelatine in it.

Cut the tips off 8 of the cooked asparagus spears
and set them aside for the garnish. Put the rest of the
asparagus in the liquidizer. Add the hot dissolved
gelatine and blend until quite smooth. Push through a
sieve, season carefully to taste and leave to cool.

Whip the cream lightly and fold it into the cool
asparagus purée. Divide the mixture between the
ramekins and put them in the refrigerator to set.

To serve, run a knife around the edge and with a
sharp tap turn out the mousses on to serving plates.
Put an asparagus tip on top of each one and garnish
discreetly with salad.

SALADE DE PRINTEMPS AUX ASPERGES ET AU GRUYÈRE

Asparagus is lightly cooked, the tips set aside for the salad and the tails liquidized with the salad dressing ingredients for extra flavour.

Serves 6
6 white asparagus spears, peeled
or 12 green asparagus spears, trimmed
mustard, salt, pepper
250 ml/9 fl oz/1 cup oil
5 tbsp vinegar
1 shallot, finely chopped
2 tbsp natural yoghurt or sour cream
plenty of chopped chives
selected interesting saladstuffs (oakleaf, lamb's lettuce/corn salad, dandelions, hearty lettuce, radiccio etc.)
100 g/4 oz Gruyère, cut in fine strips
4-5 chive flowers for decoration (optional)

Cook the asparagus in boiling salted water until just tender (12-15 minutes). Cut off the top 10 cm/4 inches and set aside. Put the tail ends in the liquidizer with the mustard, salt, pepper, oil, vinegar, shallot and yoghurt or cream. Blend to a smooth, creamy dressing; sieve if necessary.

Dress the salad in some of the dressing, then arrange on a serving dish. Split white asparagus tips in half lengthwise; leave green whole. Toss asparagus tips and cheese strips in the remaining dressing and arrange them on top. Dismember the chive flowers (if used) and scatter over the salad. Serve with *kugelhopf au lard* (p.36).

TARTE CHAUDE AUX ASPERGES

A recipe for asparagus quiche from chef Albin Brate of Restaurant Mayer in Village-Neuf, in the heart of the asparagus gardens of the Haut-Rhin.

Serves 6-8
250 g/9 oz shortcrust (basic pie) pastry
1 kg/2 lb asparagus (white or green)
250 ml/9 fl oz/1 cup double (heavy) cream
250 ml/9 fl oz/1 cup milk
4 eggs
salt and pepper

Heat the oven to 200°C/400°F/Gas Mark 6. Roll out the pastry to fit a 30-cm/12-inch quiche tin, line with foil and beans and bake blind for 10 minutes until the pastry is just set and dry, but not coloured. Remove the foil and beans and continue baking for another 5 minutes.

Peel white asparagus; trim ends of green asparagus. Cook either sort in boiling salted water for 10 minutes until barely tender. Drain and refresh in cold water. Cut off the top 7.5 cm/3 inches of each asparagus spear and reserve. Put the tails in the liquidizer or food processor with the cream, milk, eggs and seasonings. Purée till smooth, then sieve to remove fibres.

Pour the asparagus cream into the pre-baked pastry shell, arrange the asparagus spears on top like the spokes of a wheel and bake for 35-40 minutes until the custard is set and golden brown.

Variation: strips of ham (100 g/4 oz) can be added to the custard.

Tarte chaude aux asperges

THE BREADMAKER'S
CRAFT

In Alsace there is a great deal more to baking than *baguettes*. To step inside a good baker's shop is like taking a step back into history: Roman, Germanic, Austrian, French, Polish and Jewish influences are all there. Beautiful gnarled, free-standing *pains paysans* made on a leaven system from a combination of wheat and rye rub floury shoulders with the all-white *sous-brot* or 'penny loaf', curiously folded and quartered. *Petits pains au lait* (milk rolls) with their characteristic dimpled shape vie for shelf space with others, brown and white, speckled variously with poppy, sesame or caraway seeds.

Kugelhopfs, said to have come to Alsace from Austria via Marie-Antoinette, line the windows like hats in a milliner's shop. At times the familiar turban shape gives way to other forms: a star for Christmas, a crayfish for a marriage, an infant bundle for a baptism, a bunch of grapes for the harvest. Each festival has its own special bread or cake: *beignets* for carnival, paschal lambs for Easter, fat little St Nicholas figures (*Männala*) with currant eyes for 6 December, Three Kings bread (*galette des Rois*) for Epiphany. Christmas brings *bredle* (Christmas biscuits/cookies), and the sticky, gooey *Berawecka* or pear bread, as black as the best Christmas pudding.

Perhaps most tempting of all are the shiny brown salt-studded *bretzels* with their soft and chewy texture. Their name is said to be derived from the Latin *bracchium* or arm, presumably a reference to the crossed arms inside their oval shape. Theirs is a simple dough, rolled out to thin snake-like shapes, formed into

30

elaborate figures of eight, dunked alarmingly into a solution of caustic soda and sprinkled with coarse salt just before baking. The *bretzel* shape is claimed as the emblem of the Alsace bakers' corporation and crops up regularly on the intricate wrought iron signs outside the best bakers' shops.

Before bakers had their own ovens, it was the *fourniers* (oven-keepers or parish bakers) whose job it was to take their own and others' risen loaves to be baked at the manor house or nearby monastery. Gradually they built their own ovens and the profession of baker as we now know it began to evolve. Later, people built ovens on to the outside of houses, particularly in the Sundgau (southern Alsace) where many are still in regular use: Madame Hell in Ranspach-le-Bas once a week fans the flames of her wood-fired furnace and commits to its care sufficient loaves to feed her large and fortunate household, from great-grandmother (eighty-four this year) down to two-year-old Cindy: four generations all under the same roof.

For my beginner's course in Alsace breads, I approached the President of the Federation of Bakers and Pastry Chefs in Strasbourg, Monsieur René Matter, who referred me to his family bakery. At ten to four one Monday morning I duly found myself poring over my map of Strasbourg, puzzled to find the River Ill mysteriously on my left instead of on my right where it should more properly have been. Two policemen in a battered van drew up alongside me. I beamed engagingly and explained about my tryst with the baker, a story which they presumably found so unlikely that they felt it necessary to escort me on to the premises. Arriving on the dot of four under police guard, I found that Gaston and Bruno, my instructors for the night, had been hard at work since eleven o'clock the previous night.

Huge quantities of unbleached bread flour ('Type 55') are mixed together with yeast, water and salt in carefully prescribed proportions and the resulting dough kneaded to within an inch of its life, divided up into loaf-sized pieces and left to rise in floury, cloth-lined baskets. The risen loaves are turned out on to baking trays and slashed with a razor – here Bruno explained with touching pride that every baker will slash his loaves differently. He clearly relished the fact that *his* loaves bore his

Baker's sign in Colmar

A bread oven in the Sundgau

own distinctive stamp. There was certainly little risk of them being confused with mine when my turn came.

Once ready, the bread is slid smartly into the jaws of the oven, a sharp jet of steam goes up, the door clangs shut and about twenty minutes later the deep golden crusty loaves are retrieved with the baker's peel and cast into a large wire bin. The crust crackles and chunters at the sudden change in temperature and the smell is celestial. 'Come back and spend the night any time you like!' grinned Gaston.

My next task was to track down a recipe for *kugelhopf au lard*, the savoury (salt) version of the famous loaf where bacon and walnuts replace the usual raisins and almonds. Monsieur Marchand, my friendly neighbourhood baker in Hagenthal-le-Bas, came to the rescue. First we took flour, then yeast, butter, milk and eggs. An apprentice was dispatched to the butcher's next door to buy minutely diced bacon. A magnificent pottery *kugelhopf* mould, the outside blackened by constant use, its inner glaze a spider's web of fine cracks, was brought down from the shelf and liberally buttered. Walnut halves were placed strategically in the runnels at the bottom. Battle was ready to commence.

With one well-practised hand Monsieur Marchand

nonchalantly crumbled the fresh yeast straight into the bowl of flour, and with the other he switched on the mixing machine (which bore a reassuring resemblance to my own model). I began to feel dangerously optimistic about my chances of reproducing the loaf at home.

Next came the butter, not melted but simply massaged and squeezed into pieces between the same workmanlike fingers. Then came the lightly beaten eggs and finally some warm milk. The machine took over for a few minutes, and soon there emerged a smooth, supple ball of dough into which Monsieur Marchand deftly buried the bacon bits, dried onion flakes and finely chopped walnuts. 'Take care', he admonished, 'not to let the bacon get crisp when you fry it, otherwise it will turn into little stones in the finished bread.' With that, he took hold of the dough speckled with bacon like a teacake with raisins, pressed it roughly into the mould and left it to rise.

The *kugelhopf au lard* baked and ready, Monsieur Marchand ventured a variation on the theme: 'How about a *kugelhopf surprise*?' The thinly-sliced loaf was anointed with a cream cheese mixture and interspersed with slices of raw ham. We reassembled the whole magnificent edifice, then stood back to admire our handiwork. 'Maybe a little Muscat would slip down rather well,' he suggested, his kind pink face alight with mischief and Alsace hospitality. We sat on the floury marble slab munching our lunchtime rations before he adjourned for his well-earned baker's afternoon nap.

Monsieur Marchand et ses pains

Pains au pavot

The combination of wholemeal and rye flours with white flour gives a rustic, nutty-tasting bread which is far from heavy. Shape into rolls or a loaf as you wish.

Makes about 16 rolls or 1 large loaf
300 g/10 oz/2 cups plain (all-purpose)
white flour
100 g/4 oz/1 cup wholemeal (whole wheat)
flour
100 g/4 oz/1 cup rye flour
2 tsp salt
15 g/½ oz fresh (compressed) yeast
or 7 g/¼ oz instant-blending (rapid rise)
dry yeast
50 g/2 oz/4 tbsp butter
300 ml/½ pint/a generous cup milk (or milk
and water)
2-3 tbsp poppy seeds

Mix together the flours and salt. Sprinkle the dry yeast (or crumble the fresh yeast) on to the flours, add the butter and work it in, as if making pastry. Add enough milk (or water and milk) to make a firm and not too sticky dough. Knead vigorously until smooth and springy. Leave to rise until doubled in bulk. Knock down and roll up into a sausage. Shape rolls as above and put them on a greased baking sheet; or press the dough into a lightly greased loaf tin. Allow to double in bulk once more.

Heat the oven to 220°C/425°F/Gas Mark 7. Just before baking, spray the rolls or loaf with water and sprinkle with poppy seeds. Bake rolls for about 25 minutes; a loaf for 30-35 minutes.

Petits pains au lait

Delicious, dimpled milk rolls for breakfast or supper with a bowl of soup; stale rolls can be used to make Bettelmann *(page 79).*

Makes 12 rolls
500 g/1 lb/3½ cups plain (all-purpose)
white flour
15 g/½ oz fresh (compressed) yeast
or 7 g/¼ oz/2 tsp instant-blending (rapid rise)
dry yeast
1 tbsp sugar
2 tsp salt
50 g/2 oz/4 tbsp soft butter
about 300 ml/½ pint/a generous cup milk

Mix together the flour, yeast, sugar and salt. Work in the butter, add the milk and knead well to a smooth firm dough. Allow to rise in the bowl until doubled in bulk.

Knock down the dough, flatten it and roll it up into a large sausage. Cut into 12 equal sized pieces each weighing about 75 g/3 oz. On an unfloured marble slab, roll them about under slightly cupped hands until each forms a nice ball. Place on a lightly greased baking sheet, and with the side of your hand slice a deep valley right down the middle almost to the bottom. Leave to rise for about 30 minutes, or until doubled in bulk. Heat the oven to 200°C/400°F/Gas Mark 6 and bake the rolls for 20-25 minutes until golden brown.

KUGELHOPF AU LARD

A rich bacon and onion loaf baked in the characteristic kugelhopf *shape; bake it in an ordinary bread tin for lack of the traditional mould.*

Serves 8-10
500 g/1 lb/3⅓ cups plain (all-purpose) white flour
15 g/½ oz fresh (compressed) yeast
or 7 g/¼ oz/2 tsp instant-blending (rapid rise) dry yeast
1 tsp salt
150 g/5 oz/10 tbsp unsalted butter
3 eggs
about 200 ml/7 fl oz/scant cup milk
125 g/4½ oz finely diced smoked bacon
1 small onion, finely chopped
or 2 tbsp freeze-dried onion flakes
12 walnut halves

In a large mixing bowl (use the electric mixer if you have one), combine the flour, yeast and salt. Bash the butter about a bit if necessary to soften it, then drop it bit by bit into the flour. Mix the eggs with a fork and add them also, together with enough milk to give a rather soft and sticky dough.

Beat very thoroughly for at least 10 minutes. It should start to come away from the sides of the bowl; if not, add sprinkles of flour as necessary until it does. Cover and leave to rise in the bowl for about 1½ hours; it should double in bulk.

Meanwhile, sweat the bacon bits gently in a heavy pan without extra fat. Do not allow them to brown. Lift them out with a slotted spoon; if using fresh onion, fry it briefly in the residual bacon fat. Grease a 20 cm/8 inch (top diameter) *kugelhopf* mould really

well, especially around the central stalk. Place a walnut half in each of the runnels at the bottom of the mould; finely chop the rest.

Knock down the risen dough and work in the bacon, onion and remaining walnuts. Turn the dough into the prepared mould, cover with a cloth and allow it to climb to above the rim of the mould – about a further hour.

Bake in a 200°C/400°F/Gas Mark 6 oven for 40-45 minutes, or until the top is golden brown and the loaf sounds hollow when tapped. Turn out to cool on a rack. Serve in slices to accompany a glass of Alsace wine, or with soup or cheese for supper.

KUGELHOPF SURPRISE

Thin slices of the preceding kugelhopf au lard *are spread with cream cheese, overlaid with prosciutto, cut in wedges and then reassembled. Often served in Alsace at wedding receptions or cocktail parties.*

Enough for at least 20 people
1 *kugelhopf au lard*
150 g/5 oz cream cheese with garlic and herbs
300 ml/½ pint/a generous cup *fromage blanc*, quark or sour cream
200 g/7 oz wafer-thin raw ham (e.g. prosciutto)

Take a thin slice off the top of the *kugelhopf*, complete with its walnuts, and set it aside. Slice the rest of the loaf horizontally into 16 *thin* slices. Leave a base (about 2 cm/¾ inch thick) on which to sit it all. Pair up the slices in the order in which they were cut. Mash the garlic cheese into the *fromage blanc* (or

Kugelhopf surprise

quark or sour cream) and spread a thin layer on one of each pair of slices. Top with some ham, spread a little more cheese on top and then sandwich it with its partner. You should have 8 'sandwiches'.

Put the reserved base on a serving plate. One by one, starting with the biggest, put each 'sandwich' on a flat plate or board and cut evenly into 8 or 16 wedges, depending on whether you want large or small mouthfuls. Then slide the cut 'sandwich' off the plate or board and on to the base. Continue cutting the 'sandwiches' into wedges and building up the layers until you have rebuilt the *kugelhopf* to its former glory. Place the nutty crown on top.

It can be prepared one day ahead, completely covered with clingfilm and refrigerated until just before demolition.

FOIE GRAS

Foie gras is an emotive subject. Sidney Smith's oft-quoted idea of heaven was eating it to the sound of trumpets, while Charles Gérard, who described the goose as 'that admirable machine which elaborates and produces the succulent substance known as *foie gras*', could clearly conceive of no other reason for the bird's existence. People concerned to defend the rights of animals doubtless think differently.

The term means literally 'fat liver', a state of affairs brought about in geese or ducks by feeding them more than they would ordinarily eat if given a say in the matter, greedy though they undoubtedly are. The technique of stuffing geese and ducks was mastered by the Egyptians: tombs dating back to 2500 BC show the bird being held by the neck and forcibly fed. The Greeks and Romans followed suit: Metellus Pius Scipio recorded in 52 BC that geese were kept in the dark for the delicate process and the favoured diet was figs. Nero, when not feeding Christians to the lions, fed himself *foie gras*. The Romans presumably brought their secrets with them when they occupied Alsace, after which the practice mysteriously disappeared for many centuries. The goose being to the Jewish diet as pork to the gentile, it was probably Alsace's large Jewish population who surreptitiously kept alive the *foie gras* know-how. Nowadays, Israel is one of the largest producers of fat livers, along with Eastern Europe. There is some production on an artisan level in Alsace.

People who profess to a sense of anti-climax on eating '*foie gras*' may not have actually had the real thing. Perhaps it was vaguely cylindrical, came out of a

A fine, fat goose liver

tin and should never have been allowed to masquerade under the noble name. Other products, euphemistically named *mousse*, *bloc* or *parfait de foie gras*, are equally disappointing. The best *foie gras* – arguably the only one worth eating and certainly the only sort you will find in a high-class restaurant – is called variously *foie gras frais*, *foie gras en terrine*, even *foie gras frais à la cuiller* if spooned rather than sliced from the terrine in which it was cooked. It is prepared from whole goose or duck livers, carefully measured salt and pepper, and possibly a smattering of spirit. It is then baked very gently and minimally in a bain-marie: too much heat and the whole thing melts into a rather expensive mistake. A good slice will be a pinkish-beige colour; a light marbling will show where the liver was carefully and patiently pieced together again after the meticulous de-veining process.

Pâté de foie gras is another story altogether, and one over which a certain confusion reigns. Alsace lawyer Marius Veyre claims to have the definitive version in his *Histoire merveilleuse du pâté de foie gras de*
Strasbourg et de ses fabricants* (the marvellous history of *pâté de foie gras* and its makers). It appears that the first *pâté de foie gras en croûte* (as it was then known) was created in 1780 by a pastry chef named Jean-Pierre Clause, native of Dieuze in Moselle and working in the service of the Marquis de Contades, then governor of Alsace. The night before the arrival of some notable guests, the Marquis informed Clause that he had had enough of rabbit with noodles and the eternal *Knefs alsaciens* (potato gnocchi). What he wanted was some real French cooking!

Clause cudgelled his brains and rose to the challenge with the idea of a cylindrical pastry case (slightly resembling an English raised pork pie) lined with a *farce* of finely diced veal and pork fat inside which were buried the whole fat livers. The masterpiece was crowned with a pastry lid and baked in a cool oven. The fat in the *farce* served as gentle lubrication, the *foies* inside their protective casing were cooked to perfection. So impressed was Contades that he despatched one forthwith to Louis XVI, who promptly rewarded the good Marquis with a piece of land in Picardy, and Clause with twenty pistols. The latter subsequently left the Marquis' service, married the widow of a *pâtissier* (presumably to secure a lifetime's supply of pastry) and devoted himself for the next forty-three years to the fabrication of the famous pies.

The truffles came later, the idea of a certain Nicolas-François Doyen, at which point the title was suffixed with the words: *aux truffes de Périgord*. Later, Brillat-Savarin listed it (along with *choucroute garnie*) as one of those supreme dishes before which no well-organized man could do otherwise than tremble and bend the knee.

Today, the undisputed *foie gras* king in Alsace is chef Schillinger of Colmar, through whose capable hands 3000 kilos of the stuff annually pass. A *Maître-Cuisinier de France*, he travels the world as a sort of roving *foie gras* ambassador: friends of ours recently caught up with him at the Intercontinental in Djakarta where he was responsible for a meal which must have astonished Indonesian businessmen and brought tears to the eyes of homesick Frenchmen. Schillinger expresses a strong preference for eating *foie gras* raw, thinly shaved onto freshly-made toast whose heat softens it into a delectable ointment. Alternatively he slices it, studs it with coarse salt and pepper and then sears it briefly on each side in a non-stick pan: *foie gras à l'ombre.*

As to which bird gives the better *foie gras*, not to mention whether it should be available at all, opinions are sharply divided. Some claim that goose wins on sheer smoothness of texture and of taste; others that duck, rather gamier and stronger-tasting, is preferable. Both have been described as 'arguably the most delectable food known to man'. It is a subject on which everyone has to make up his or her own mind.

Chef Schillinger's pâté de foie gras en croûte

41

FOIE GRAS EN TERRINE

The raw fat liver is de-veined, carefully seasoned, packed into a terrine and baked very gently and briefly.

Allow about 100 g/4 oz foie gras per serving
a fat liver (goose or duck)
15 g/½ oz/2 tsp salt per kg/2 lb liver
3 g/scant ½ tsp white pepper per kg/2 lb liver
a pinch of sugar
optional: 1 tbsp port or cognac per kg/2 lb liver

Weigh the liver. Calculate the amount of salt and pepper needed, weigh or measure it out and set aside.

Peel away any fine film surrounding the liver, as far as is feasible. Separate the two lobes and break the liver into several pieces so as to expose the veins. Remove as many as possible with the point of a sharp knife. Remove also any green bits. Put the pieces of liver in a dish, sprinkle with the measured salt and pepper, add the port or cognac and leave to marinate for a couple of hours.

Pack the pieces of liver into a terrine just big enough; it should be rather a tight fit. Press it down extremely firmly, otherwise it will fall apart when sliced.

Put sheets of newspaper in a deep bain-marie and place the terrine on top. Pour in water to come up to the rim of the terrine.

Bring the water temperature to 70°C/160°F and bake the terrine in a 110°C/225°F/Gas Mark ¼ oven. Allow 50 minutes cooking time per kg/2 lb for goose; 40 minutes per kg/2 lb for duck. Remove from the bain-marie and allow to cool very slowly.

Serve with toasted brioche and a late harvest Pinot Gris or Gewurztraminer.

ESCALOPES DE FOIE GRAS AUX POMMES REINETTES

Sliced, sautéd fat liver with apples, one of the most traditional hot foie gras dishes in Alsace, typically served at Christmas.

Serves 4
a 500 g/1 lb fat liver (goose or duck)
salt and pepper
flour
4 small dessert apples (e.g. Reinette, Cox, Jonathon)
25 g/1 oz/2 tbsp butter
a wineglass Gewurztraminer
(or ½ glass port)
a wineglass veal or chicken stock
a nut of butter

Peel away any membrane surrounding the liver and cut away any greenish parts. Separate the two lobes of the liver and remove the main vein. Cut slanting slices from each lobe. Season and dust with flour. Set aside.

Peel, core and slice the apples. Cook them gently in the butter for 5-6 minutes, turning once or twice, until just tender but not mushy. Arrange on serving plates and keep warm in the oven.

Just before serving, heat a non-stick pan rather ferociously (no fat) and sear the *foie gras* slices for about 30 seconds on each side. Put them on the warmed serving plates. Tip away the fat and deglaze the pan with the Gewurztraminer or port. Reduce a little, then add the stock and reduce again almost to a glaze. Whisk in the nut of butter, pour the sauce over the *foie gras* and serve at once.

POT-AU-FEU DE FOIE D'OIE AU GROS SEL ET MIGNONETTE DE POIVRE

Pot au feu seems to crop up in many different guises in Alsace. Chef Schillinger's version consists of foie gras wrapped in spinach leaves, steamed gently and served with tiny vegetables.

Serves 6 for a first course
a 600 g/1¼ lb fat goose liver
salt and pepper
6 beautiful spinach leaves
6 baby carrots with 2 cm/1 inch greenery left on
6 baby turnips with 2 cm/1 inch greenery left on
6 spring onions (scallions)
250 ml/scant ½ pint/1 cup well-flavoured beef stock
coarse salt and white peppercorns

Divide the *foie gras* into medallions of 100 g/4 oz each. Season them and set them aside. Blanch the spinach leaves, drain, refresh and pat them dry.

Lay a spinach leaf in a small soup ladle or rounded spoon, press a piece of *foie gras* rather firmly into it and fold the leaf over the top. Lift out the package and enrobe the remaining *foie gras* pieces in the same way.

Steam the packages for 5 minutes. Meanwhile cook the vegetables in boiling salted water until just tender. Serve a *foie gras* parcel in the middle of each hot plate, with the vegetables and some warm stock. Serve the coarse salt and roughly pounded peppercorns in a little bowl.

LIBERTE, EGALITE ET CHOUCROUTE!

'Only a stomach that seldom feels hunger scorns things common', observed Horace in a satirical moment. While many would dispute that *choucroute* has anything common about it, most would agree that for a genuine *choucroute garnie* tottering under its astonishing burden of sausages, bacon, pork chops, ham and steamed potatoes, a hearty appetite is an essential requirement.

The exact origins of this particular pickle are uncertain, though there are whispers of an oriental background. Sixteenth- and seventeenth-century cookbooks refer to something called *Gumbostkrut* or *Compostkraut*, though it is probable that this was some sort of cooked pickle rather than raw salted cabbage. Seventeenth-century monks feasted regularly on it, as did fine

Monsieur Sutter removing the tronçon

Strasbourg families on Sundays. (The story is told of a devout and distracted housewife who put the *choucroute* on to cook before going to Mass, absent-mindedly slipped her missal into the pot and rushed off to church clutching a slab of bacon in its place.) After 1800 it was relegated to a mere Tuesday dish, though its general popularity during the nineteenth century was still such that its appearance on wedding menus was almost mandatory. François Voegeling in *La gastronomie alsacienne* notes innocently that it experienced a sudden and unaccountable fall from favour between the time of the Prussian occupation of Alsace and the end of the Second World War.

Choucroute is at the heart of things *alsacien*, a symbolic dish which sets the place somehow subtly apart from the rest of France. A recent political pamphlet in which the author lambasts *alsaciens* for their meek acquiescence with orders from Paris is entitled '*Tais-toi et mange ta choucroute*' – 'shut up and eat your *choucroute*'. Baptisms or wakes, returning prodigal sons or daughters, visiting dignitaries or foreign friends may all provoke the production of a *choucroute garnie*. The Alsace autumn is punctuated by a series of *fêtes de la choucroute*, the most bizarre of which was an attempt in Turckheim in 1989 to concoct the 'biggest *choucroute* in the world' for the *Guinness Book of Records*. There was some debate as to whether or not it qualified for the title, but a good time was had by all.

Choucroute is made in the autumn on the silage principle. A special variety of tightly packed white cabbage is shredded finely and layered with salt in a large crock, then left until it ferments (about three weeks). Sometimes it is necessary to add a little water, but generally the lactic acid released by the action of the salt on the sugars in the cabbage is enough to cover and preserve it through the winter. Though some people still make their own, most content themselves with buying it on an *ad hoc* basis from the butcher or direct from the producer. As it is hardly worth embarking on the process with less than 50 kg (110 lb) of cabbage, you need to have either a huge, hungry family, or be prepared to follow the example of the monks of the Middle Ages and eat it at least once a week. Another disincentive, as Tom Stobart observes in his *Cook's Encyclopaedia*, is that 'making it at home can be rather smelly'. The same process is also applied to the large white turnips of the area to give *navets salés*.

Roger Lallemand in *La vraie cuisine de l'Alsace* maintains that '*choucroute* is *alsacienne*. Otherwise it isn't *choucroute*.' Two things distinguish it from simple *sauerkraut*. One is the use of wine in the cooking, preferably an everyday-quality Riesling – the ultimate insult in Alsace is to describe something (or someone) as being 'as bland as *choucroute* cooked in water'. The other is the richness and variety of the garnish: meats, sausages, sometimes even liver dumplings. Controversy rages – for *choucroute* leaves nobody indifferent – over the correct length of the cooking time: some claim that the cabbage should retain a suspicion of crunch, others that the vegetable should be quite soft and a mellow golden colour. (True *alsaciens* claim that *choucroute* is really only any good when reheated at least seven times.)

As eating habits change, however, and families get smaller, such dishes are an endangered species. In an attempt to boost flagging consumption, the professional *choucroute* body has recently undertaken an impressive national campaign for the product, stressing its nutritional properties (it is an excellent source of vitamin C, a fact appreciated by Captain Cook and his scurvy-threatened sailors) and its low calorific value (it's the sausagery which does the damage). Chefs have also done their bit to revive the image; Guy-Pierre Baumann, a famous expatriate *alsacien*, long ago conquered Paris with his *choucroutes aux poissons*, in which the use of fish rather than meat for the garnish is less modern than you might suppose; one of the many celebrated dishes served by Emile Jung at Le Crocodile consists of thin slices of pike-perch sandwiched with a little wine-braised *choucroute* and a white butter sauce.

But the real defender of the *choucroute* faith must be Toni Hartmann of Oltingue. A little while ago he sat in his restaurant deep in the Sundgau with a group of fellow chefs, all of them reflecting mournfully on *choucroute's* fall from favour. As the Riesling flowed freely, the ideas became ever more fantastic. Thus was conceived the *Confrérie de la Choucroute*, a society for the preservation of pickled cabbage. Their terms of reference: to reverse its alarming decline in popularity by devising intriguing recipes which attempt to rid it of the heavy, peasant food image under which it unjustly labours. Their battle cry: *Liberté, Egalité – et Choucroute!*

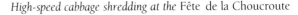

High-speed cabbage shredding at the Fête de la Choucroute

CHOUCROUTE GARNIE A L'ALSACIENNE

Try to find a really good selection of smoked sausagery and pork for this dish, layer the meats with the choucroute, *moisten with white wine, put in the oven and then go off for a good long walk to work up an appetite.*

Serves 6 hungry people

1½ kg/3 lb raw *choucroute* (fresh, canned or bottled)
2 onions, finely chopped
2 cloves garlic, mashed
1 tbsp lard, bacon fat or goose fat
400 g/14 oz smoked bacon in one piece
750 g/1½ lb salted or smoked pork loin
400 g/14 oz salted belly pork (side pork) or forehock
1 bayleaf
8 juniper berries
4-5 coriander seeds
2 cloves
pepper
½ litre/1 pint/2 cups dry white wine (e.g. Riesling)
½ litre/1 pint/2 cups water or stock, more if necessary
6 large baking potatoes, peeled
6 Strasbourg sausages (*Knacks*) or frankfurters
3 Montbéliards or other smoked boiling sausages

Wash the *choucroute* in several changes of cold water and squeeze it out well.

In a large ovenproof casserole, into which everything will eventually fit, soften the onions and garlic in the fat. Put in half the *choucroute*, add the smoked bacon, pork loin and the belly pork or forehock; cover with the rest of the *choucroute*. Bury the bayleaf, juniper berries, coriander seeds and cloves amongst the meat and vegetables, season well with pepper, moisten with the wine and water or stock and bring to a gentle simmer.

Bake in a 180°C/350°F/Gas Mark 4 oven for 1½-2 hours. Top up with stock or water if the liquid evaporates too soon. Meanwhile cook the potatoes until just tender. Prick the sausages and let them heat through in a pan of hot water. Do not boil or they will burst apart.

Arrange the *choucroute* on a large, hot serving plate. Slice meats and pile them and the sausages and potatoes on top of the *choucroute*. Serve with plenty of mustard, and a good everyday Riesling.

SALADE DE VOLAILLE TIEDE A LA CHOUCROUTE

A light, piquant dish from the founder of the Confrérie, Toni Hartmann of L'Oltinguette, Oltingue: pieces of chicken breast are tossed in butter and served over a warm choucroute salad.

Serves 4
4 small chicken breasts (half breasts), each about 80 g/3 oz
salt and pepper
1 tbsp oil
250 ml/9 fl oz/1 cup chicken or veal stock
75 g/3 oz/6 tbsp butter
150 g/5 oz raw *choucroute*
chopped chives

Dice and season the chicken breasts. Toss briefly in hot oil, then keep warm. Discard the oil and deglaze the pan with the stock. Let it reduce almost to a glaze, then whisk in 50 g/2 oz/4 tbsp of the butter.

Rinse, drain and squeeze dry the *choucroute*. Toss it in another frying pan in the remaining butter for a few minutes until the *choucroute* is hot but barely cooked. Arrange it on serving plates, scatter the chicken on top, spoon a little sauce over each one, scatter with chives and serve.

QUICHE A LA CHOUCROUTE

Monsieur Fischer at the Studerhof in Bettlach takes the familiar choucroute/charcuterie combination, folds it into a light custard and encases it all in a fine pastry crust: an excellent way to use up leftovers from a choucroute garnie.

Serves 6-8
200 g/7 oz puff pastry
100 g/4 oz smoked streaky (fatty) bacon, diced
100 g/4 oz salted belly pork (side pork), diced
4 eggs
300 ml/½ pint/a generous cup milk
200 ml/7 fl oz/scant cup double (heavy) cream
salt and pepper
800 g/1¾ lb cooked *choucroute* (see *choucroute garnie*)

Roll out the pastry and line a 30-cm/12-inch diameter quiche tin. Chill. Fry the bacon and belly pork gently in a heavy pan until the fat runs. Degrease on paper towels. (If you have some bacon and belly pork left over from a *choucroute garnie*, use them; no need to fry them.) Mix together the eggs, milk, cream and salt and pepper to taste. Stir in the bacon, pork and *choucroute*.

Heat the oven to 220°C/420°F/Gas Mark 7. Tip the filling into the pastry case and bake the quiche for 45 minutes or until set and golden. Serve lukewarm.
Note: for a quiche for 4 people, halve all quantities and bake in an 18-cm/7-inch quiche tin.

FEUILLETE AUX DEUX SAUMONS A LA CHOUCROUTE

An original recipe from Monsieur Pierre Wabnitz, Le Cheval Blanc, Tagolsheim: slices of fresh and smoked salmon layered with choucroute *and wrapped in puff pastry.*

Serves 4

4 escalopes of fresh salmon about ½ cm/¼ inch thick (about 75 g/3 oz each)
½ wineglass Riesling
2 shallots, finely chopped
a little butter
about 200 g/7 oz raw *choucroute*
150 ml/5 fl oz/⅔ cup chicken or fish stock
350 g/12 oz puff pastry
4 thin slices smoked salmon
1 egg yolk
250 ml/9 fl oz/1 cup fish stock
100 ml/4 fl oz/½ cup white wine
a wineglass of double (heavy) cream
juice of 1 lemon

Marinate the salmon escalopes in the Riesling with one of the shallots for 2 hours in a cool place. Rinse and squeeze dry the *choucroute*. Soften the second shallot in a little butter for a few minutes, then stir in the *choucroute*. Moisten with stock and cook gently for 30 minutes or until barely tender.

Roll out the pastry to a large rectangle and trim all the edges. Cut into four pieces. At one end of each piece, place an escalope of salmon, followed by a thin layer of *choucroute* and a smoked salmon slice. Paint the pastry border with water, fold the uncovered pastry over, press the edges together to seal. Decorate with pastry trimmings, make a steam hole, glaze with beaten egg yolk and chill for at least 2 hours or until needed. Bake in a preheated 220°C/425°F/Gas Mark 7 oven for about 15 minutes or until the pastry is golden brown.

For the sauce, boil the fish stock down to reduce by half, then add the wine and reduce again. Whisk in the cream and reduce again. Check the seasoning, sharpen with a few drops of lemon juice and serve with the *feuilletés*.

Note: can be prepared ahead.

Feuilleté aux deux saumons à la choucroute

THE CHARCUTIER'S ART

*Without [the pig] there were, in truth,
an acting void and an empty cuisine . . .*
GEORGE ELLWANGER, *PLEASURES OF THE TABLE*, 1903

Throughout Alsace's long and well-chronicled gastronomic history, the pig has always enjoyed a privileged position. The Romans, no mean pork butchers
themselves, were so impressed with the hams, sausages
and *cervelas* of the people of the left bank of the Rhine
that they promptly set up a brisk trade with the capital of
the Roman empire.

During the Middle Ages, pigs (curiously, often owned
by bakers) were allowed to graze freely in the streets of
Strasbourg. Eventually both pigs and bakers got a bit out
of hand, the former wreaking havoc in the unpaved
streets, the latter encroaching on the *charcutiers'* territory. In the end the bakers were confined to making
bread and only pigs owned by the Antonine monks were
allowed to roam loose in the streets, on condition that
they were branded with the Tau cross, the sign of the
order.

Somehow, St Antony manages to reconcile his roles as
patron saint both of pigs and of pork butchers: he is
often depicted on wrought-iron butchers' signs, such as
the beautiful one in Colmar designed by Hansi which
shows him reading to an attentive beast. In the
magnificent Issenheim Altarpiece at the Musée Unterlin-
den, a couple of cheerful-looking piglets peep out from
under his protective robes. His name has given us the
word 'tantony', the smallest pig in a litter.

But it is to the Benedictine monks once again, in
matters gastronomical, that Alsace has reason to be

extremely grateful; when they were not making wine for communion, brewing up *eaux de vie* (strictly for medicinal purposes), making Munster to mop up excess milk production, or rearing snails to lighten the long Lenten fast, they were busy converting their pigs into all manner of delicacies for the monastery table, and incidentally laying the foundations of Alsace's rich and varied *charcuterie* tradition.

Under Louis XIV, as a special favour from the Sun King – *'il ne faut pas toucher aux affaires d'Alsace'* ('Alsace affairs should not be interfered with') – the free grazing rights (pannage) enjoyed by pigs throughout the region's many forests were extended. Some claim that this fact helps to explain the unusually highly developed state of the pork butcher's art in Alsace: a free-range pig is not only more succulent, he is also less vulnerable because

he does not depend on man for his fodder, and has a better chance of eluding the axe when times are hard.

Few families in Alsace wield the axe nowadays. If they own a pig at all, they will call on the local butcher to lend his services for the *cochonnailles* (slaughter and sausage-making ceremonies) which are still something of a feature of the Alsace autumn. First the cuts to last through the winter are salted and set aside, then the bits which do not keep are made into sundry sausages for instant consumption. The whole thing provides the perfect pretext for a party, with lashings of newly salted *choucroute* and copious quantities of *neia Siassa*, the newly fermenting wine.

Perhaps the best party dish of all is a *jambon en croûte*, a whole succulently braised ham sliced and skilfully reassembled, parcelled up with string and buried in bread dough. Baked to a rich brown on the outside, the crust soaks up the gently seeping juices from the inner ham, rendering superfluous any accompaniment other than salad.

Other noble by-products of the pig are the Alsace *pâtés*, forty-two varieties of which were eloquently described by the nineteenth-century writer Charles Gérard in *L'ancienne Alsace à table*. Some are intricately moulded in pastry or encased in boned birds; others are rolled up, bolster-like, in a crust, or simply baked *en terrine*. Ingredients may range from noble *foie gras* to humble rabbit; sweetbreads, wild boar, venison, pheasant or duck may each play a part. But the main ingredient will always be pork in one form or another; lean cuts for lightness, fat pieces for juiciness, sheets or cubes of back fat to lubricate the whole.

Should you stray as far south as St Louis, make a bee-line for the Hertzog butchery. Monsieur Hertzog not

Butcher's sign in Colmar, by Hansi. Previous page: Family and staff at the Boucherie Hertzog, St Louis

only heads the local Federation of Butchers and *Charcutiers* (the professions are linked in Alsace), he also represents France in the International Confederation and at the EC in Brussels. Luckily for the locals, he still finds the time to mastermind the making of an outstanding range of sausages, smoked meats and pâtés which are ably marketed by Madame Hertzog and her team. Customers are greeted like long-lost friends, enquiries are made after the family, special orders are noted, advice is given as to a particular cut of meat required for a special dish, good wishes offered for the success of the occasion. Upstairs in the kitchen Jean-Paul busies himself with *pâtés en croûte*, *tourtes*, tarts, salads, noodles and *spätzle*, canapés for parties and a whole range of 'convenience foods' without which no self-respecting St Louis housewife would contemplate running a household.

GLOSSARY OF ALSACE SAUSAGERY

Presskopf/tête or *fromage de porc* – brawn (head cheese), finely diced pig's head set in a clear savoury jelly; eat cold with vinaigrette.

Blutwurscht/boudin – black pudding (blood sausage), made of blood, pork, rinds, onions and spices; heat and serve with apple sauce or boiled potatoes

Schwarzwurscht/saucisse noire – smoked black sausage, composition similar to black pudding; slice thinly and eat cold

Knacks/saucisses de Strasbourg – similar to frankfurters and made from pork and veal; poach or grill (broil)

Bratwurscht/saucisses à frire – frying sausages, can be made from pork (like Toulouse sausages), or veal; texture varies from fairly coarse to very fine

Landjaeger/gendarmes – flat sausage of beef and pork; can be eaten raw or cooked into a soup

Hiriwurscht – smoked pork and beef sausage typical of the Sundgau, eat raw or stir into a hot soup or vegetable purée

Mettwurscht/saucisse à tartiner – sausage spread made of pork, beef and spices

Klepfer/cervelas – fat, dumpy pork and beef sausage; can be fried, grilled (broiled), heated in a soup or eaten cold in a salad

Lawerwurscht/saucisses de foie à tartiner – sausage spread made of pork liver

Spack/lard – belly pork (fresh side pork), fresh or salted or bacon, salted and/or smoked

Schunke/jambon – ham of various sorts

Schieffala/épaule – pork shoulder salted and smoked, to accompany *choucroute*; sometimes boned and rolled to roast and served with horseradish sauce and potato salad

PATE CHAUD ALSACIEN

An easy-to-make, bolster-shaped pâté en croûte *made of pork and veal which can be served hot or cold. Great on a buffet table.*

Serves 8-10
500 g/1 lb boneless pork shoulder (or similar cut)
500 g/1 lb boneless veal shoulder (or similar cut)
400 g/14 oz canned, sliced mushrooms
100 g/4 oz/4 slices stale bread soaked in milk
salt and pepper
2 tbsp finely chopped onion or shallot
4 tbsp finely chopped parsley
200 ml/7 fl oz/scant cup double (heavy) cream
500 g/1 lb puff pastry
4-5 eggs, hard-boiled
1 egg, beaten

Finely chop or process together the meats. Chop the mushrooms. Squeeze out the bread. Beat both into the meats, with salt and pepper, onion or shallot, parsley and cream; chill the mixture if time permits.

Roll out the pastry to a rectangle. Lay half the meat filling in a line along one edge of the pastry, arrange the eggs on top and cover with the remaining meat; smooth into a sausage shape with wet hands. Paint the edges of the pastry with beaten egg and bring it up and over to enclose the meat. Cut away any excess and tuck the edges under to form a nice fat bolster. Decorate with pastry trimmings. Place on a lightly greased baking sheet and glaze with beaten egg. Bake for 1 hour in a 200°C/400°F/Gas Mark 6 oven or until the pastry is golden brown and the meat cooked. A skewer stuck in the middle of the pâté should be hot. *Variation:* make a mini-pâté using half quantities of everything, and quails' eggs instead of hens'.

SPAETZLE

A sort of primitive pasta, and the classic accompaniment for game in Alsace. Butchers sell them ready made, and the Hertzogs' version are especially good and light because of the fromage blanc. *They are easy to make at home and freeze well.*

Serves 6
250 g/9 oz/1¾ cups plain (all-purpose) white flour
50 g/2 oz/⅓ cup fine semolina
1 tsp salt
3 eggs
125 g/4½ oz curd (farmer's or pot) cheese (*fromage blanc*)
4 tbsp finely chopped fresh herbs (optional)
about 6 tbsp water

In the electric mixer or food processor, mix together the flour, semolina, salt, eggs, curd cheese and optional herbs or spinach. Add just enough water to give a soft, dropping consistency, like cake batter. Leave to rest 30 minutes.

Bring a large pan of salted water to a gentle boil. Tilt the bowl over the pan (use rubber gloves, or you may scald yourself), allowing the mixture to come just to the lip of the bowl. Slice off ribbons of batter into the water by sweeping a very sharp knife across the lip of the bowl.

Repeat the process several times, then wait till the *spätzle* float to the surface. Remove them with a slotted spoon to a colander, rinse in cold water and spread out on a tea(dish)-towel to dry.

Continue with the rest of the mixture. Toss in hot butter just before serving.

BAECKEOFFE

Lunch on the day I was invited to work behind the scenes at the Hertzog butchery in St Louis featured this classic dish of pork, beef, lamb and potatoes, marinated in white wine.

Serves 8

500 g/1 lb each of boneless stewing pork,
shoulder of lamb and stewing beef (e.g. skirt)
2 pig's trotters (feet)
1 tbsp salt
lots of freshly ground black pepper
a sprig of thyme
2 bayleaves
2-3 cloves garlic, mashed
lots of chopped parsley
2 tbsp finely diced celeriac
½ bottle dry white wine (preferably an Alsace
Riesling)
1½ kg/3 lb firm, waxy potatoes, peeled
and sliced
2 medium onions, chopped
2 small leeks, sliced

Cut the meat in bite-sized pieces and put in a large non-metal container with the pig's trotters. Toss with the salt, pepper, herbs, garlic, parsley and celeriac and moisten with the wine. Cover and leave in a cool place overnight.

Grease lightly a large ovenproof casserole with lid. Put the pig's trotters in the bottom and cover with half the potatoes, onions and leeks. Lift the meats out of the marinade and put on top. Cover with the remaining vegetables. Pour on the reserved marinade and add enough extra wine or water to bring the liquid barely to the top of the vegetables.

Cover the casserole and seal the join between lid and pot with a paste made from 125 g/4½ oz/a scant cup flour mixed with 5 tablespoons water and a tablespoon of oil. (Alternatively use heavy-duty foil and the lid.) Bake in a 200°C/400°F/Gas Mark 6 oven for 1 hour; lower the heat to 180°C/350°F/Gas Mark 4 and bake for a further 1½ hours. The meats should be tender and melting and the potatoes just cooked.

Serve straight from the dish (trotters are reserved for the real enthusiasts) with plenty of salad, crusty bread and a bottle of the wine used for the marinade.

TOURTE VOSGIENNE

*A sort of creamy pork quiche with a pastry top,
which makes an excellent supper dish or picnic
pie. Can be served warm or cold; it reheats
beautifully.*

Serves 4-6
500 g/1 lb boneless pork shoulder or similar cut
1 tbsp finely chopped shallot
2 tbsp finely chopped parsley
salt and pepper
125 ml/4½ fl oz/½ cup dry white wine (Riesling
or similar)
25 g/1 oz/2 tbsp butter
400 g/14 oz puff pastry
1 egg yolk
200 ml/7 fl oz/scant cup double (heavy) cream
2 eggs

Cut the pork in finger-sized strips and mix in a bowl
with the shallot, parsley, salt, pepper and wine. Leave
to marinate overnight. Next day, toss the pork strips
in hot butter for a couple of minutes to stiffen.

Cut the pastry in half and roll out one half to a
circle slightly larger than a 26-cm/10-inch quiche tin.
Line the tin with it, leaving an overhanging border of
about 2 cm/1 inch all around. Scatter the pork pieces
over the pastry. Roll out the other piece of pastry to
make a circle big enough to cover the pie and border.
Wet the overhanging border of the bottom pastry, lay
the second piece of pastry on top, trim to fit and press
the joined edges together to seal. Bring them up and
over to form a rolled edge around the circumference
of the pie. Cut a hole in the top, paint with beaten egg
yolk, mark with a fork and bake at 180°C/350°F/Gas
Mark 4 for 20 minutes.

Mix together the cream, eggs and salt and pepper.
Remove the pie from the oven and pour the mixture
through the hole in the roof. Bake for a further 15
minutes to set the custard.
Variation: instead of pork strips marinated and tossed
in butter, use left-over strips of ham or *Schieffala*
(page 71).

JAMBON EN CROUTE

*This dramatic and delicious party dish comes
from Boucherie Wimmer in Hésingue.
Sometimes the ham is wrapped in bread
dough (as here) sometimes in puff pastry.
Serve with salads.*

Serves 16-20
a 4-5 kg/9-11 lb boneless ham
2 onions stuck with cloves
2 carrots
1 leek
bouquet garni
peppercorns
double quantity brown bread dough (*pains
au pavot*, page 35, or *pain
paysan* page 86)

The day before you plan to serve it, put the ham in a
large casserole with the onions, carrots, leek, bouquet
garni, peppercorns and water to cover. Bring to the
boil and simmer very gently for 30 minutes per half
kilo/pound. Allow to cool in the liquid.

Next day, make up double the quantity of bread
dough for *pains au pavot* or *pain paysan* and
allow it to rise in the bowl. Lift the ham out of the
stock and cut away the skin and excess fat. Slice it
down almost to the bottom and if necessary tie some

string loosely around it to stop it flapping about. Knock down the risen dough and roll or pat it out about ½ cm/¼ inch thick. Sit the ham on a doubled sheet of foil (which prevents excess seepage into the dough) and envelop it in the dough. Seal the joins (which should be underneath) with water and tuck under any excess dough. Put on a lightly greased baking sheet and bake at 200°C/400°F/Gas Mark 6 for about 30 minutes; reduce the heat to 180°C/350°F/Gas Mark 4 and bake for a further 1½ hours or until the dough is a rich golden brown and sounds quite hollow when tapped. Cover the crust with foil if it is colouring too much.

To serve, cut into the dough near the bottom and lift the crust off. Extract slices as best you can and serve each with a slice of crust.

Jambon en croûte

SNAILS, SYLVANER AND SNAKES

Pinned to many a tree in forests throughout Alsace is a small notice declaring that the gathering of snails (and other goodies) is forbidden, by order of the Mayor. We had always suspected a cartel, but never managed to have the suspicion confirmed. Imagine my delight, therefore, on reading an article entitled *L'Eloge de l'escargot*, to find that the author of this astonishing snail panegyric was a Monsieur Rieb, Secretary General to the Mayor of Barr. Proof at last? I wrote suggesting an interview. A courteous note returned, confirming that Monsieur Rieb had effectively served as right-hand man to the Mayor during many years, was indeed a noted

Gros Bourgogne *snails after an autumn shower*

lover of snails, but had retired some fifteen years previously, and unfortunately died in 1983. The snail trail had dried up once more; research continued apace.

Snails have always been popular in Alsace. From the Romans the people learned the secrets of snail husbandry, in particular how to fatten them on selected titbits in specially designed *escargotières* or snaileries. Irène Kohler in *La cuisine alsacienne* reports that by the Middle Ages monasteries and convents (notably the Clos des Capucins near Kaysersberg, now home of Madame Faller) were famous for their snails. Charles Gérard in *L'ancienne Alsace à table* remarks understandingly that the winters were so long, and the Lenten fast so trying that it was little wonder that snails played such a large part in the monastic diet.

According to Monsieur Rieb's article, snails have a uniquely finely tuned sense of smell, which – knowing the alacrity with which they home in on my freshly planted basil – I have no difficulty in believing. In the village of Osenbach, near Guebwiller, there is an annual Fêtes des Escargots.

Snail races take place, in the course of which I am told that these remarkable beasts have been known to log speeds of over a hundred metres an hour. Such unseemly haste, however, is apt to have disastrous results: an over-exercised snail is apparently a tough proposition. (Presumably the racing snails are kept in separate quarters from the ones which are subsequently consumed in industrial quantities.)

The best time to gather snails is in the autumn before they have had a chance to clock up much mileage, and after a good rainstorm which brings them out of hiding. Reputedly best of all are the *gros Bourgognes*, also known as Roman snails or *Helix pomatia*. The limestone soils on which they thrive aid the building of their magnificent chalky shells.

Their consumption is not, however, confined to the autumn and throughout the year snails are collected, cooked and eaten with disconcerting gusto (especially by Mayors). They are served in many different ways, not just with the usual garlic butter: one restaurant in Ribeauvillé manages to incorporate them into no fewer than nine different dishes: for starters you could have snail soup, with snail brioches or *kugelhopf* for dunking therein, or a modicum of scrambled eggs with snails. Also tempting is the snail *feuilleté*. To follow, maybe a small snail casserole, or for the more adventurous a *tarte flambée* with snails. More substantial would be home-made pasta with snails and spinach, while snail custards or a snail quiche could usefully plug any gaps.

There is some debate as to which wine is the most suitable accompaniment. An interesting suggestion came from Monsieur Jean Meyer, of JosMeyer in Wintzenheim, in the course of a tasting of his excellent wines. First came a Sylvaner. As we sniffed, slurped and sighed contentedly, he announced, in his deliciously accented English, that this was without doubt the best wine to accompany a dish of snakes. There was a stunned silence. 'Snakes?' we echoed, aghast. 'Yes,' he insisted, 'Sylvaner is vairy wonderfool with snakes, I 'ave served it once at a banquet of Monsieur Gaertner's in Ammerschwihr.'

For a moment, I wondered if chef Gaertner had come up with an interesting little dish for his autumn menu at Aux Armes de France, and made a mental note to call him to see if he would be prepared to divulge the recipe. Then the penny dropped. We got snails and snakes straightened out and continued to savour the Sylvaner. Monsieur Meyer, something of a poet by nature and by now warming to his subject, encouraged us not to scorn this usually unloved grape, which on the right soil and with the right vinification can produce an excellent, fruity wine. He made much of its deliciously fresh, green, *grassy* nature. 'Perfect for snakes', I ventured. Doubt flickered briefly across his usually cheerful face, followed instantly by a broad grin. *Touché*!

POT-AU-FEU D'ESCARGOTS A L'ETOILE D'ANIS

Snails are served here in a little stew, with tiny vegetables. A recipe from Patrick Fulgraff, Le Fer Rouge, Colmar, one of Alsace's most talented young chefs.

Serves 4
125 g/4½ oz each baby turnips, carrots and courgettes (zucchini)
75 g/3 oz mangetouts (snow peas)
100 g/4 oz cauliflower
2 dozen canned snails, rinsed and drained
300 ml/½ pint/generous cup beef stock
2 star anise
50 g/2 oz/4 tbsp soft butter
salt and pepper
optional: 75 g/3 oz chanterelles or other mushrooms
sprigs of chervil

Trim and cut the turnips, carrots and courgettes (zucchini) into neat ovals. Trim the mangetouts (snow peas) and cut the cauliflower into flowerets. Cook each vegetable in boiling salted water until barely tender. Drain and refresh in cold water.

Simmer the snails in the stock for 10 minutes. Remove and keep them warm. Infuse the star anise in the stock for 5-10 minutes, then reduce by one third. Whisk in the soft butter to emulsify and thicken slightly. Check the seasoning.

Fry the chanterelles (or other mushrooms) in a little butter for 7-10 minutes or until just cooked, then add the remaining vegetables and toss over moderate heat until really heated through.

Arrange the snails, vegetables and mushrooms on warm soup plates, pour the stock over, sprinkle with chervil sprigs and serve at once with crusty bread.

CASSOLETTE D'ESCARGOTS AU RIESLING

From Chef Guggenbuhl at La Taverne Alsacienne in Ingersheim comes this delectable creamy snail soup with mushrooms, garlic and herbs.

Serves 6
6 dozen medium canned snails
2 shallots, chopped
1 clove garlic, mashed
25 g/1 oz/2 tbsp butter
300 g/10 oz mushrooms, wild (chanterelles, pleurotus, boletus, morels etc.) or cultivated, sliced
salt and pepper
125 ml/4½ fl oz/½ cup Riesling
125 ml/4½ fl oz/½ cup veal or chicken stock
300 ml/½ pint/generous cup double (heavy) cream
finely chopped parsley, chives and chervil
croûtons

Rinse the snails and drain. Soften the shallots and garlic in the butter, then add the sliced mushrooms and salt and pepper to taste. Cook gently for 5 minutes, then raise the heat to evaporate the moisture. Deglaze with the wine, add the snails and simmer 5 minutes. Add the stock and allow to reduce by half. Whip the cream and stir it in. Simmer for about 5 minutes more, then serve in heated soup bowls lavishly sprinkled with chopped herbs and crusty croûtons.

ESCARGOTS EN RAVIOLE AUX GRAINES DE PAVOT

Ravioli of snails with poppy seeds. Fine pasta is stuffed with a pork, veal, cabbage and snail farce and served with the reduced cooking juices. Recipe from François Kiener, Auberge du Schoenenbourg in Riquewihr.

Makes 36 ravioli, serving 6-8
300 g/10 oz pasta dough (see page 136)
3 dozen canned snails, medium size
250 ml/9 fl oz/1 cup chicken stock
6 tbsp dry white wine
salt and pepper
150 g/5 oz cabbage, finely chopped
150 g/5 oz belly pork (fresh side pork)
150 g/5 oz boneless lean veal or pork
a dash soy sauce
1 tsp finely chopped chives
3 tbsp poppy seeds
1 shallot, finely chopped
3 tbsp parsley, chopped
50 g/2 oz/4 tbsp butter
1 tbsp oil
125 ml/4½ fl oz/½ cup whipped cream

Make up the pasta dough as usual with the flour, salt, eggs and oil. Leave to rest.

Rinse the snails and poach them for 10 minutes in the stock and wine with salt and pepper to taste. Allow to cool in the stock.

Sprinkle the cabbage with salt and leave in a colander to drain. In the food processor chop the meats finely. Squeeze out the cabbage to remove any moisture and add it with the soy sauce, chives, 1 tablespoon poppy seeds, shallot and parsley to the meats. Process again until well mixed. Season to taste.

Cut the pasta dough in half and roll out one half as finely as possible. Place teaspoons of filling at regular intervals all over the dough and bury a snail in each one. Wet all the spaces between the mounds of filling with water. Roll out the second piece of dough and lay it over, pressing down between fillings to seal the two layers of dough. Cut out ravioli. Freeze if not for immediate consumption.

Heat a little butter and the oil in a large wide pan and fry the ravioli on one side only. Remove as they are ready to an ovenproof dish. Add snail stock to almost cover and bake them in a 200°C/400°F/Gas Mark 6 oven for 10-15 minutes. Remove and keep them warm. Tip the stock into a pan, add another tablespoon of poppy seeds and reduce to a sticky glaze. Whisk in the remaining butter and at the last minute the whipped cream. Arrange the ravioli on heated plates around a small mound of cooked shredded cabbage sprinkled with remaining poppy seeds. Drizzle some sauce over and set an empty snail shell on top of the cabbage mound.

Escargots en raviole aux graines de pavot

THE *FERMES AUBERGES* OF THE HIGH VOSGES

It is a truth universally acknowledged that the only possible reason for embarking on some really strenuous exercise is to build up an appetite for a good meal. For many years now *fermes auberges* throughout the Vosges have obliged by providing copious meals for ravenous, red-stockinged, red-faced walkers, or blue-nosed cross-country skiers. Though the casual visitor may feel that his need for sustenance is all-important, the fact is that the principal purpose of the hill farms is and always has been agricultural: *'Fermier d'abord, aubergiste ensuite, voilà notre devise!'* affirms Monsieur Jean Wehrey, President of the *Association des Fermes Auberges du Haut-Rhin* – 'farmers first, innkeepers second, that is our motto!'.

Though some farms are occupied all year round, others – particularly those high up in the Vosges – are only inhabited during the summer. An evocative account in the Journal of the Industrial Society of Mulhouse describes how around 25 May (St Urbain) the beautiful old cow bells are taken down and burnished, the beasts bathed and their tails trimmed before the long walk up to their summer quarters. The oldest cow goes first – she knows the way by heart. Their delight at the fresh, lush grass at the top after the fusty, musty winter hay is not hard to imagine. Shutters, doors and windows are opened, a great celebration of summer begins.

Once the family have tended to their own and to their cows' needs, it is the turn of the hungry walkers. In summer there may be chairs and tables set out on a rudimentary 'terrace' in the farmyard, while winter rations will be served in a large, simple room lined with benches and long refectory tables. There is usually no question of booking or of ordering: you simply stagger over the doorstep, find a seat and take whatever is offered.

Typically on offer is the *repas marcaire* or 'dairyman's meal' (*marcaire* comes from the dialect *meliker*, meaning the milker of cows). First may come a *tourte de la vallée de Munster*, a flaky-crusted pork pie served warm with a green salad, likely in the spring to include dandelions picked in the wake of the receding snows. Then comes a joint of smoked pork with the unpronounceable but entirely delectable *roïgabragelti*, a sort of potato hash with onions. The etymology is uncertain and its origins also disputed; according to some it came from the Bernese Oberland with the many Swiss who repopulated Alsace after the Thirty Years War; others claim that it was ever a favourite dish of the foresters and charcoal-burners of the Vosges, cooked in the embers of their dying fires.

A home-grown Munster cheese follows, served with or without cumin seeds (frowned on by the purists, hailed by others as the essential antidote to indigestion), and finally a *meringue glacé* of impressive proportions or a bilberry tart which blackens the teeth beautifully, served with lashings of whipped cream. Blue-grey stoneware jugs of Edelzwicker are quaffed in quantity and an *eau de vie* distilled from almost any of the many fruits and berries which grow in the Vosges helps to shake things down before the walk home.

If you arrive early enough and show an interest, you may be introduced to the cows and taken through the cheese-making process. Although records exist of Munster fabrication dating back to the days of Charlemagne, it was the Benedictine monks who perfected the art of cheese-making in the Vosges. Nowadays it is the prerogative of the hill farmers, and Munster is one of twenty-seven French cheeses to enjoy its own *appellation*

contrôlée which limits the cheese's production to a clearly defined area.

The evening's milk is left to stand all night, then skimmed the following morning. To it is added the morning's milk and the whole is heated together to just under blood heat. Rennet is added, the milk turns, and the whole mass is cut into pieces with a spatula. The curds are then pressed into Munster moulds, the whey fed back whence it came.

The cheese in its fresh virginal state is sometimes offered as a dessert, bathed in whipped cream, drenched with kirsch and sprinkled with sugar: *Siesskäs*. *Bibeleskäs* is fresh, lightly salted Munster mashed with garlic and cumin and served with boiled potatoes for supper. Cheeses for maturing will be salted and ripened, either by the farmer or by an *affineur* such as Monsieur Haxaire in Lapoutroie.

His job is to turn and brush the cheeses with water over a period of about three weeks, a process which favours the growth of the right bacteria and gives them the characteristic orangey Munster hue. '*Le fromage*', he says with relish, in a memorable phrase which would give most Ministers of Health nightmares and indigestion, '*c'est un bouillon de cultures!*' ('cheese is a veritable cauldron of bugs!'). Munster has a penetrating odour of old socks which belies its relatively mild taste.

Some *fermes auberges* offer overnight accommodation, such as the one we booked into once in early May. Winter had lingered late that year, and from the tone of Madame Lochert's voice it was clear that she questioned the wisdom of the scheme, particularly given the lack of central heating at the farm. Nothing daunted, we set off up into the Vosges. For every hundred metres of height

Spring flowers (grow in abundance) in the Vosges

gained, it seemed that we lost about ten degrees of heat. By the time we arrived, it was snowing gently. We began to wonder whether Madame might not have a point.

We pushed open the front door. In the corner of the dining room crouched a huge tiled stove which radiated welcome waves of heat. Madame appeared from the kitchen, wiping her hands on the tea-towel fixed to her apron. Would we like to see the room before dinner? We followed her out, obediently clutching our bags, trying not to gasp at the contrast in temperature between the cosy dining room and the arctic staircase. In the bedroom we could see our breath; one of the children etched a snowman with a fingernail in the ice on the inside of the window.

We crept gratefully back down to the warmth of the dining room and feasted on the welcome *ferme auberge* fare. As dinner wore on, recollections of the temperature in the upstairs room played obstinately around the edges of the mind and chilled the body. We held a whispered consultation. My husband took a deep breath, rose and explained in his best and most apologetic French to Madame that the dinner had been outstanding, the welcome warm, but the temperature . . . he spread his hands helplessly. Madame didn't actually say 'I told you so'. In fact she was all kindness and comprehension. The children, on the other hand, by now engaged in a full-blown snowball fight and enjoying themselves hugely, howled with disappointment. We fled upstairs once more to grab our bags, promised we'd be back later in the summer and beat a hasty and rather undignified retreat back to Basle. Never have a hot bath, central heating and a warm bed felt better.

Sunday lunch at the Ferme auberge *Lameysberg*

SCHIEFFALA (PALETTE DE PORC) ET ROIGABRAGELTI

Smoked pork shoulder with an unctuous potato casserole, a ferme auberge classic and great fare for hungry walkers. The recipe comes from Madame Wehrey (wife of the Association's President) of the Ferme Auberge Buchwald, near Metzeral.

Serves 6
1 kg/2 lb salted boneless smoked pork
shoulder
stock or water
optional: a little white wine
2 tbsp lard or oil
1 kg/2 lb firm (boiling) potatoes, peeled and
sliced
100-200 g/4-7 oz/1-2 sticks butter
1 large or 2 small onions, finely chopped
salt and pepper

Soak the shoulder in cold water to remove excess salt. Put in a pan with water or stock (and wine if used) to come two-thirds of the way up the meat. Cover and simmer very gently for about 1 hour or until tender when pierced with a fork.

Heat the lard or oil in a large heavy casserole (preferably cast iron). Put in half the sliced potatoes, follow with half the diced butter, half the chopped onions and salt and pepper to taste. Add the remaining potatoes and the rest of the butter, onions and seasoning. Start off the casserole over a brisk heat, until you can hear protesting noises coming from beneath the potatoes and little wisps of steam are visible. Reduce the heat to moderate and cover the casserole. Cook for about an hour, and then test the potatoes to see if they are done. If not, give them a bit longer. Once they are cooked, turn the heat up once more and stir the contents of the casserole up to mix thoroughly. Serve with the pork, with plenty of good mustard and a green salad.

SALADE DE PISSENLITS AU LARD ET AUX OEUFS DURS

A classic salad whose warm crunchy bacon bits contrast pleasingly with the slightly astringent dandelion leaves. Substitute any winter salad, such as curly endive or corn salad if you prefer, or if your supply of dandelions is a bit skimpy.

Serves 6
about 500 g/1 lb dandelion leaves
3 hard-boiled eggs
150 g/5 oz smoked streaky (fatty)
bacon, diced
3 tbsp vinegar
pinch sugar
salt, pepper
vinaigrette (optional)

Wash and dry the dandelion leaves (or other salads). Put in a large bowl with the finely chopped eggs. Fry the bacon dice until the fat runs. Lift out the bacon and scatter it over the salad.

Whisk the vinegar, sugar, salt and pepper into the fat in the pan and pour it over the salad. Serve at once with extra vinaigrette if wished.

TOURTE DE LA VALLEE DE MUNSTER

A spiced pork forcemeat is baked in a quiche tin, shortcrust pastry underneath and puff on top. Super for an informal lunch dish, or for a picnic.

Serves 6-8
100 g/4 oz/2½ cups stale bread, crumbled
6 tbsp milk
2 medium onions, finely chopped
2 cloves garlic, mashed
25 g/1 oz/2 tbsp butter
850 g/1¾ lb boneless, slightly fat pork, cubed
salt and pepper
1 tsp mixed spice (apple pie spice)
4 tbsp chopped parsley
2 eggs
300 g/10 oz shortcrust (basic pie) pastry
225 g/8 oz puff pastry

Mix the bread with the milk and leave to soak. Soften the onions and garlic in the butter without browning. Chop or process the pork fairly finely. Squeeze out the bread and mix it into the meat with the onions, garlic, salt, pepper, spices and parsley. Beat the eggs up with a fork and keep some back to glaze the pie. Add the rest to the meat and beat or process well to lighten the mixture.

Roll out the shortcrust pastry for the base to a large circle rather bigger than a 26-cm/10-inch quiche tin. Lay it in the tin, allowing an overhang of about 3 cm/1¼ inches all around. Heap the pork mixture on top, doming it up towards the centre. Brush the exposed pastry border with water. Roll out the puff pastry for the lid, again a little larger than the tin, and place it on top. Trim it to match the bottom piece of pastry. Press the two borders together to seal, then bring them up and over to form a rolled border all around the circumference. Prick or cross-hatch with the point of a sharp knife and make a hole in the top as a safety valve.

Preheat the oven to 200°C/400°F/Gas Mark 6, paint the pie with the reserved beaten egg and bake for 45 minutes to 1 hour: the pastry should be golden brown and a skewer stuck in the middle will feel uncomfortably warm to the cheek. Remove from the oven and let it rest at room temperature for at least half an hour before eating. It is usually served warm, but is equally good cold.

TARTE AUX MYRTILLES

*Bilberry tart, for which the season begins in the Vosges in the second half of
August and continues till the end of September. Blackberries could be substituted.*

Serves 6
200 g/7 oz sweet shortcrust (basic pie) pastry
2-3 tbsp fresh breadcrumbs
about 500 g/1 lb bilberries
6 tbsp double (heavy) cream
4-5 tbsp sugar
1 tbsp flour
2 eggs

Roll out the pastry to fit a 26-cm/10-inch quiche tin
and bake blind. Sprinkle with the breadcrumbs, add
the bilberries and bake in a 200°C/400°F/Gas Mark 6
oven for 15 minutes. Whisk together the cream,
sugar, flour and eggs. Remove tart from the oven and
pour on the cream mixture. Return to the oven for a
further 15-20 minutes or until the custard is set.
Sprinkle with icing (confectioners') sugar if wished
and serve tepid.

THE BUNNERS OF BENNWIHR

'Kugelhopf un Tarte
D'Schulde kenne warte!'

'With kugelhopf *and pie*
you can wave your debts goodbye!'
ALSACE PROVERB

We crossed the courtyard behind the Bunners' house and pushed open the door of what was to be our home for a week. Sitting smugly on the kitchen table was a freshly baked *kugelhopf* of magnificent proportions, its crown studded with almonds and lightly dusted with fine sugar. 'I do hope you'll be happy here', beamed Madame Bunner.

We had rented a gîte (self-catering holiday flat) in the village of Bennwihr. The suffix *wihr*, common throughout this part of Alsace, comes from the Latin *villa*; Bennwihr (*Villare Bebonis*) was evidently the chosen spot of Bebo, probably a Roman soldier or civil servant who had become attached to the area in which he served and later chose to stay. Close to Colmar and in the heart of the Haut-Rhin, the village enjoys one of the best micro-climates in the area: one of its sunniest hillsides is called the Mandelberg, where privileged vines grow.

Throughout the week, Monsieur Bunner went about the daily business of tending the vines. Madame Bunner also helped in the vineyards, returning every midday to cook lunch for the children home from school and Granny upstairs. Spare moments were spent in her exemplary allotment: serried ranks of leeks, onions, beetroot and beans jostled for space with courgettes (zucchini), tomatoes and saladstuffs, all for summer consumption. For winter stores there were potatoes, carrots and tight white cabbages destined for *choucroute*.

In a drawer in the kitchen of the *gîte* we found a book entitled *Un village martyr au coeur de la poche de Colmar: Bennwihr 3-24 décembre 1944*. Compiled in 1981–2 by a group of pensioners who feared that 'their young people did not even know why their village was new', it is a heartrending, first-hand account of the final moments of the war, when Bennwihr became a martyred village trapped in the infamous Colmar pocket. The Allies were all around. On 20 November 1944, Mulhouse was liberated, Strasbourg on the 24th. Soon it must be the turn of Bennwihr.

When the bombs started falling, on the evening of Sunday 3 December, the surprise was near total. One villager relates that she was making butter, another that she was kneading bread and realized there would be no time to bake it. Another keenly regretted the recent slaughter of the family pig, destined for the pâtés with which she had intended to regale the liberating troops. They fled down into the cellars, consoling themselves that in a couple of days it would all be over.

A couple of days turned into a week, then two. At the beginning, there were pauses in the bombardment which enabled brave *cave*-dwellers to surface to milk the miraculously surviving cow or to bring provisions from those few houses which remained standing. Later, as intermittent shelling became a hail of bombs, hope of a quick resolution to the combat dwindled. The cellars housed – indiscriminately – French, Americans, even Germans, civilian and military, religious and secular.

Ironically, considering they were sheltering in the wine cellars, the worst problem was one of thirst, for there had been no time to prepare supplies of drinking water. The *Schnapps* distilled in preparation for the long-awaited liberating troops was used as fuel to heat for the babies what little milk could be gleaned on snatched visits to the cowshed.

Finally, on 14 December, the order was given by the Germans to evacuate the village. Granny Bunner recalls that they made a ragged band as they emerged from the cellars in their clogs or house slippers, filthy dirty and flea-ridden, the men unshaven, the women unkempt. Pushing what belongings still remained to them in wheelbarrows normally used for taking fodder to the cowshed, they picked their grisly way through the corpses and dismembered limbs towards the muddy road and the relative safety of nearby Ingersheim. In February 1945, after the liberation of Colmar, they returned to smoking ruins populated by only a few hens, pigs and goats. Visiting the site after the war was over, de Gaulle remarked simply: *'Je n'ai vu nulle part chose pareille'* ('Nowhere have I ever seen anything like this').

But the people of Bennwihr (known as *Mondfänger*, those who bay for the moon) have a special reputation for resilience. By 1946 rebuilding was already well underway with the construction of the co-operative to which the Bunners now belong. Nowadays, except for the fact that Bennwihr is conspicuously modern where other villages and nearby towns are jewels of medieval architecture, a huge effort of imagination is required to conjure up those last days of 1944. Only the inscription on the *nécropole*, set amid the vines on the crest of the hill called Blutberg above Bennwihr, serves as a chilling reminder that Alsace was not always the warm, happy, prosperous, well-fed place it is today:

On these foothills of the Vosges, in this plain of Alsace, in deep snow and temperatures twenty degrees below zero, the soldiers of France, Africa and the United States, united in the First French Army under the orders of General de Lattre de Tassigny, won through to a resounding victory in the bitter struggle of the Battle of Colmar, 20 January-9 February 1945.

KUGELHOPF

A light raisin and almond bread, kugelhopf makes gorgeous dunking material for the breakfast coffee or hot chocolate. In the old days, the dough was beaten vigorously with the hands; nowadays Madame Bunner uses her electric mixer.

Serves 6

500 g/1 lb/3⅓ cups plain (all-purpose) white flour
5 tbsp sugar
a pinch of salt
7 g/¼ oz/2 tsp instant-blending (rapid rise) dry yeast
or 15 g/½ oz fresh (compressed) yeast
150 g/5 oz/10 tbsp soft butter or margarine
2 eggs, lightly mixed
about 200 ml/7 fl oz/scant cup warm milk
100 g/4 oz/⅔ cup raisins
2 tbsp kirsch or hot water
8-10 unskinned almonds
icing (confectioners') sugar in a shaker

In the electric mixer bowl, mix together the flour, sugar, salt and yeast. Work in the butter as if making pastry. Mix together the eggs and milk and add also. Beat hard for at least 5 minutes until the dough starts to come away from the sides of the bowl. Add sprinkles of flour if necessary to achieve this state of affairs.

Allow to rise in the bowl for as long as it takes to double in bulk (1½-2 hours). Soak the raisins in the kirsch or water.

When the dough has risen, punch it down and incorporate the raisins. Butter a *kugelhopf* mould thoroughly and put an almond in each runnel. Press in the dough, cover with a cloth and leave to rise again until doubled.

Heat the oven to 200°C/400°F/Gas Mark 6 and bake the loaf for about 45 minutes, or until it is golden brown on top and sounds hollow when tapped. Turn it out: if it is still a bit pale inside, return it unmoulded to the oven for 5-10 minutes more. Leave to cool on a rack, then sprinkle with icing (confectioners') sugar just before serving.

SALADE DE BETTERAVES

When you are faced with a glut of beetroot, take a tip from Madame Bunner: cook, peel and freeze them so that in winter you can have beetroot salad on hand all the time.

Serves 4
8 small beetroot (beets), cooked, peeled
and diced
salt and pepper
300 ml/½ pint/a generous cup oil
100 ml/4 fl oz/½ cup vinegar
1 tbsp mustard
pinch sugar
chopped chives
2 hard-boiled eggs, chopped

Season the beetroot and put in a serving dish. Whisk together the oil, vinegar, mustard, sugar and salt and pepper to make a smooth emulsion. Spoon some over the beetroot and sprinkle with chives and chopped hard-boiled eggs.

Salad de betteraves

BEIGNETS DE COURGETTES

*These courgette (zucchini) fritters were
devised by Madame Bunner as a delicious
way to accommodate those courgettes which
grew by mistake into marrows.*

Serves 4-6 as an accompaniment
1 large courgette (zucchini) or 2 medium
(about 450 g/1 lb), grated
1 tsp salt
3 eggs
freshly ground pepper
2 tbsp chopped parsley and chives
1 shallot, finely chopped
3 tbsp flour
oil or clarified butter

Place the grated courgettes (zucchini) in a colander,
sprinkle with the salt and leave to drain for at least an
hour. Squeeze them out well and discard liquid. In a
large bowl, mix together the eggs, pepper, herbs,
shallot, flour and grated vegetable.

Heat oil or clarified butter to a depth of ½ cm/
¼ inch in a large frying pan and shape little
(5-6-cm/2-inch diameter) fritters using a slotted
spoon. Slide them off the spoon into the hot fat and
fry until really golden and crusty on both sides,
creamy in the middle.

BETTELMANN

A very traditional dessert a bit like clafoutis,
often made with stale kugelhopf *(above) or
milk rolls,* petits pains au lait *(page 35).*

Serves 6
4 slices *kugelhopf*, or 3 stale milk rolls (about
150 g/5 oz)
400 ml/14 fl oz/1¾ cups warm milk
½ tsp vanilla essence (extract)
3 eggs, separated
100 g/4 oz/½ cup sugar
a pinch of salt
3 tbsp kirsch
300 g/10 oz black cherries, stoned (pitted)
or 4 apples, peeled, cored and chopped

Steep the stale bread in the milk until soggy. Then
process or mix it together with the vanilla, egg yolks
and all but 2 tablespoons sugar. Beat the whites with
the salt until stiff but not dry, sprinkle on the
remaining sugar and continue beating until stiff and
glossy. Fold this into the bread mixture, and stir in
the kirsch. Add the cherries or apples and pour into a
greased 24-cm/9½-inch quiche tin or gratin dish.
Bake at 200°C/400°F/Gas Mark 6 for 40-50 minutes or
until golden brown and firm. Serve tepid or cold, with
real vanilla ice cream.

CHEESE AND WINE IN
THE SUNDGAU

The *Sundgau* is the southern part of Alsace (*Sund*=south, *gau*=district) and stretches from Mulhouse to the Swiss border, from the river Largue across to the Rhine. It resembles no other part of the province, with its gently rolling hills, rich forests, wide open spaces and distant, tantalizing gimpses of the Jura, the Vosges, the Black Forest and – on exceptionally clear days – of the Alps. Previous landlords have included the House of Hapsburg and the Bishopric of Basle; artists and poets have long found inspiration in its beautiful landscapes and picturesque villages with their polychrome half-timbered houses (blue for Catholics, ochre or salmon pink for Protestants), many of which have now been preserved for posterity in the Eco-Musée d'Alsace at Ungersheim. A glance at the map shows a huge concentration of ponds, rich source of the area's most famous dish, fried carp, which can be freely sampled all along the *route des carpes frites*.

The Michelin green guide describes it as *un pays bien individualisé* (a very individualistic region); certainly (see also the chapters on asparagus and *choucroute*) it seems to boast a higher than average number of interesting and eccentric characters devoted to quality and authenticity, each one a mine of information about his or her own particular field. One such is Monsieur Antony, champion cheesemonger in Vieux-Ferrette. For him cheese is not merely a business, it is his life.

On Tuesdays he is to be found holding sway (usually in the Alsace dialect, for French comes reluctantly to the *sundgauvien* tongue) from his refrigerated van in a prosperous suburb of Mulhouse; on Fridays, practically by special appointment, in the courtyard of an accommodating farmer in Oltingue; and on Saturdays in the Sundgau's capital town of Altkirch. The shiny waxed paper in which your purchases are lovingly enveloped informs you that he is a member of the *Garde et Jure de l'Ordre des Fromagers de la Confrérie de St Uguzon*. This august body, named after the patron saint of cheese-mongers, was founded twenty years ago by Pierre Androüet with the aim of preserving genuine French country cheeses; *les fromages du terroir*. A fervent disciple of Androüet, Monsieur Antony stocks a selection of the very best cheeses from all over France, made exclusively from unpasteurized milk. If the relevant cows are not known personally to him (as in the case of his Munster *au lait cru*), their owners certainly are. The decision on which is the best moment to sell each one rests with him: useless to arrive with your heart set on a Coulommiers, if today the right cheese to buy is a Vacherin or a Comté. '*Le fromage*', claims M. Antony waggishly, 'is like *une belle femme*: you have to wait until the time is right.'

Monsieur Antony and his Munster man

Cheese can also be bought in the small shop adjoining his home in Vieux-Ferrette, but his real pride and joy is the *Käs-Keller* or cheese cellar where the astonishing seven-course cheese extravaganzas known as *cérémonies de fromages* are held. When the long winter evenings began to draw in, we assembled a group of similarly cheese-minded friends and signed up for a ceremony. The proceedings opened with a luscious late-harvest Gewurztraminer to accompany the tiny appetizers of potted blue cheese steeped in the same wine, a happy invention of Monsieur Antony's. We sat back in anticipation.

He introduced us first to his goats; from Provence, Corsica, Savoie, Tarn, Périgord, Touraine, ranging from chalky to creamy, from mild-mannered to assertive. A Sauvignon from the Loire turned out to be an excellent companion for them. The next plate featured Vacherin, Reblochon, Moines de Citeaux, Chambarand, Pavé d'Auge, Comté and St Nectaire, ably partnered by a bottle of Chambolle-Musigny.

Now came the turn of the soft cheeses, Brie, Coulommiers, Rigotte de Lisère and St Marcellin. We eased over from Burgundy to Bordeaux. Signs of strain were evident around the table, but at the suggestion of a little lemon sorbet to sharpen the palate, the mood brightened perceptibly. The Munster, being Alsace's only native cheese and rather a law unto itself, travelled alone. Then the lights dimmed and we watched in awe as a chafing dish of flaming Langres bathed in *marc* moved inexorably towards us out of the darkness. The final nail in the coffin was a half Stilton, procured triumphantly in our honour by Monsieur Antony from a specialist in English cheeses in distant Toulouse. He tasted it, as a *sommelier* might sample the first glass of wine before bringing it to the table. He seemed to enjoy it very much. We thought wistfully how much we might enjoy it at

Dusk in the Vosges

Christmas, six weeks hence. If one had to eat dessert at all, Madame's unforgettable fresh fruit salad was undoubtedly the best option, and a fitting climax to an unforgettable ceremony.

Unforgettable, too, are the wines to be found *chez* Freund in Hégenheim, though the very banal-looking Codec supermarket seems an unlikely place for them. Fighting your way past the *bretzel* stand and the queues of people waiting to buy lottery tickets, past the disposable nappies, the plastic plates and the fizzy lemonade, you reach the wine department. From floor to ceiling are ranged some 900 different wines from all over France, with a distinct emphasis on Burgundy, Bordeaux

Monsieur Freund at work

and the best Alsace names. In the middle of the Bordeaux section of his list comes the simple comment: 'Life is too short to drink bad wine.' Yet '69 Romanée-Contis at around 1800 french francs co-exist peacefully with litre bottles of Edelzwicker at 16.95 FF, for Monsieur Freund is well aware that for every Burgundy-loving, Swiss franc-touting Basler who has popped over the border 'to Freund's', there are hundreds of local customers concerned to supply themselves with good everyday drinking wine. In the corner of the shop is a small wine bar bedecked with half-open bottles, enthusiastically patronized by faithful clients. On Saturdays it's elbow-room only.

The Freund family came from Germany in the early eighteenth century and settled in St Louis. Successive Freunds occupied posts as Mayors, Masters of the Staging Post and brewers until in 1878 Freund et fils was founded by the uncle of the present owner. At that time they sold only bread and petrol: *pain et pétrole*. Over the years the motto has been 'to modify, not to mummify', hence the fact that today the range of foodstuffs goes far beyond bread, while petrol has

been superceded by liquids of a rather different sort. Monsieur and Madame Freund recently celebrated, respectively, fifty-three and a half and forty-six and a half years of active participation in Freund et fils: one hundred years of joint service to the community in a shop whose renown reaches far beyond the immediate confines of Hégenheim, providing an excellent excuse for a party.

To Monsieur Freund's comprehensive understanding of wine can be added a vast store of knowledge of local history and of the people who helped shape it. At a quarter past two on the afternoon of Friday 1 September 1939, he recalls, the people of Hégenheim were given four hours in which to assemble easily portable belongings and valuables, as well as provisions to last them for five days. In addition they should deposit their keys at the Mairie, switch off the water, gas and electricity and take their leave of any dogs, cats or farm animals.

At dusk they were to walk to Jettingen (some twenty kilometres/fourteen miles), from where they travelled in cattle trucks on a three-day journey across France to Morcenx in the Landes. One year later they returned to find that their houses and businesses had been ransacked, sometimes by the German troops, more often, comments Monsieur Freund with understandable acerbity, by fellow *alsaciens* who had managed to escape evacuation.

The enforced bonds forged during the wartime evacuation often developed in peacetime into a network of solid and lasting friendships, and it was Monsieur Freund who was chiefly responsible for the twinning of Hégenheim with its host village Morcenx. In 1989, fifty years on, another chapter closed as hundreds of villagers staged a 'voluntary re-evacuation' to the Landes to revisit briefly this extraordinary episode in the life of this *pays bien individualisé*, the Sundgau.

Fondue aux quatre fromages de Monsieur Antony

Drawing on his unusually fine stock of cheeses, Monsieur Antony makes this delicious version for fondue evenings in the Käs-Keller.

Serves 5-6
400 g/14 oz Beaufort
200 g/7 oz French Emmental
200 g/7 oz Gruyère
200 g/7 oz Comté
optional: 150 g/5 oz Mont d'Or du Jura
1 clove garlic
½ bottle dry white wine (e.g. a Chasselas from Savoie)
plenty of pepper
2 tbsp kirsch

Remove rinds from all the cheeses and grate finely. Rub an earthenware fondue dish with the cut clove of garlic. Add the cheeses, moisten with the wine, season with pepper and bring gently to the boil, stirring assiduously the while. Add the kirsch at the last minute and take to the table.

A 'Freund-lich' Gewurztraminer Cup

From some Gewurztraminer left over from a Freund tasting, we developed this delicious, thirst-quenching summer cup.

Makes about 1 ½ litres/2 ½ pints/6 cups
3-4 pieces each of orange and lemon zest, cut with a potato peeler
a few pieces of cucumber peel
a small sprig of mint or borage
1 tbsp sugar
2-3 tbsp marc de Gewurztraminer
(or substitute another spirit)
1 bottle Gewurztraminer
lots of ice
250 ml/scant ½ pint/1 cup fizzy mineral water

In a large jug, mix together the orange and lemon zests, the cucumber peel, the mint or borage, sugar and spirit. Leave to infuse for a while. Add the wine, plenty of ice and the mineral water. Chill well.

PAIN PAYSAN DE MADAME HELL

*Madame Hell in Ranspach-le-Bas bakes nine
or ten of these loaves in one batch in her
old wood-fired stove each week. Here is her
recipe, scaled down to make one large loaf.
It keeps well and goes beautifully with cheese.*

500 g/1 lb/3¼ cups unbleached/plain (all-
purpose) white flour
100 g/4 oz/1 cup wholemeal (whole
wheat flour
100 g/4 oz/1 cup rye flour
15 g/½ oz fresh (compressed) yeast or
7 g/¼ oz/1 tsp instant-blending (rapid rise)
dry yeast
about 350 ml/12 fl oz/1½ cups water
2 tsp salt

Mix half the flours together in a bowl. Dissolve the
fresh yeast in the water (or add the dry yeast directly
to the flours, followed by the water). Mix well to form
a rather wet batter. Leave to ferment overnight.

Next day, mix in the remaining flour and the salt
and knead well. The dough can afford to be quite wet,
but should not stick excessively to your hands. Leave
it to rise in the bowl, covered with a cloth, until
doubled in bulk (1-2 hours, depending on the
temperature of the room).

When it has doubled in bulk, knock it down, turn
it out of the bowl and knead it vigorously once more.
Line a round bowl or basket with a well-floured
tea(dish)-towel and put the dough in. Allow it to rise
once more until doubled in bulk.

Heat the oven to 220°C/425°F/Gas Mark 7. Invert
the dough on to a lightly greased baking sheet and
bake the loaf for 30-35 minutes or until it sounds
hollow when tapped. It will be rather an odd shape
with an unusually delicious flavour.

POMMES DE TERRE COIFFEES
DE MUNSTER

*Baked potatoes with melted Munster cheese.
A wickedly calorific and wonderful supper
dish, and a good way to use up odd
bits of Munster.*

For each person you need:
1 baked potato
50 g/2 oz ripe Munster cheese,
rinds removed
pepper
gherkins

Halve the baked potato and lay slices of cheese on top.
Season with pepper and put briefly under the grill
(broiler) until the cheese melts. Serve with gherkins
and a salad.

Madame Hell's pain paysan

TOWN *WINSTUBS* AND COUNTRY TAVERNS

To visit Strasbourg without ever setting foot inside a *Winstub* would be like going to London and giving the pubs a miss. These typical 'wine-bars' with their tiny tables and checked curtains are full to bursting with people feasting on inordinate quantities of simple, rustic food: snails, onion tart, Gruyère and *cervelas* salads, great slabs of ham *en croûte*, liver dumplings, *choucroute* and something called *Saümawe*, which turns out to be a sort of porky relation of haggis.

The origins of the *Winstub* can be traced back to the fourteenth-century *Stuben* or *poêles*, meeting rooms owned by the butchers' and bakers' corporations. Here they would assemble to down a glass of wine and catch up on the latest professional news. A legacy from these days is the *Stammtisch*, a special table reserved in every *Winstub* for the regulars. Ownership later passed into the hands of grower-merchants, looking for an outlet in town for their wines from the vineyard villages. Though this is sometimes still so, the owner nowadays is more likely to be some independent, enterprising soul who has managed to stamp his or her own personality on the place to such an extent that the *Winstub* is part and parcel of the person. S'Burjerstuewel in Strasbourg is just such a place. Partly because the name is entirely unpronounceable, more because of the owner herself, most people refer to it simply as '*chez* Yvonne'.

Orphaned on 16 December 1940 at the age of fourteen, Yvonne Haller fled to Paris to work as a cook. After two years she set her sights on getting to Switzerland – no easy task in 1942. Though initially

turned back at the border, she was eventually successful and embarked on a four-year stint in a restaurant in St Gallen. She recalls that with one half day's holiday per month, it was there that she learnt what hard work meant.

Meanwhile S'Burjerstuewel saw a series of owners, who were successively bankrupted. In 1954 Yvonne returned to her native Strasbourg and took over the *Winstub*. After fifteen years she allowed herself her first day off. Thirty-four years· on she permits herself the unheard-of luxury of Sunday and Monday lunchtime closing, and 'a real holiday from Bastille Day to the middle of August'.

For the benefit of those unfamiliar with the phenomenon, I asked her to define a *Winstub*. Settling her upswept spectacles firmly back on to her nose, she explains (patiently and fairly calmly, in spite of a power cut and a hundred hungry Strasburgers expected to hurtle through the door for lunch in twenty minutes' time) that it's a place where people go to eat, to be with their friends or to make new ones, to forget their problems, to relax. Parliamentarians rub shoulders with artists, bankers with off-duty chefs, tourists with locals. For Yvonne it's all a bit like a giant dinner party. She takes evident delight in engineering contact between people in an age where communication is a dying art, so you must sit where you are told and eat what the hostess suggests. Sometimes, she adds with a bit of a chuckle, it works better than others (rather like my dinner parties).

When last there I was placed next to two delightful gentlemen jewellers. We shared a jug of Pinot Noir, discussed the book, exclaimed over the success of their recent sales trip to Djibouti, and together waxed lyrical about the home-made *foie gras*, the unctuous, pinkly braised tongue with its sharp sauce of egg yolk, chopped capers and pickles, and the wicked plum tart. Out of the corner of my eye, I could see Yvonne beaming with approval.

When the days begin to shorten and the temperatures to

Invitation to step inside a Winstub

drop, the country counterparts of the *Winstubs* once again start to do a brisk business in *Flammekueche*, Alsace's answer to pizza. It consists simply of wafer-thin bread dough stretched out to the size of a large chopping board (on which indeed it is served), spread with *fromage blanc* and cream, scattered with slivers of smoky bacon and onion and baked in a wood-fired oven built into the side of the restaurant wall. The dish was originally translated into French as *tarte flammée*, a name which accurately captured the image of the flames. Unfortunately, some journalist with a fevered imagination thought that *tarte flambée* sounded more exotic, and saddled it for posterity with a name which quite erroneously suggests chafing dishes and amateur pyrotechnics at the table. Nothing could be further from the truth.

Though very much part of the northern Alsace tradition, *flammekueche* is a dish which only began to crop up in cookbooks at the end of the last century. Many families claim, however, that it is a good deal older

Right and previous page: The city of Strasbourg

Inside chez Yvonne, *Strasbourg*

than that, but that no one troubled to write it down since it developed as a simple by-product of Saturday bake-day: leftover dough (probably a mixture of rye and wheat flours) flattened out, spread with whatever was in the larder and baked hot on the heels of the bread batch, directly on the floor of the oven and licked by the rekindled flames from the huge logs (hence the *flamme* part of the *kueche*). It was a 'brunch' dish, served to father when he came in from his early labours, usually preceded by a hearty soup and accompanied by a tot of *eau de vie*, mid-morning being considered 'too early for wine'.

A l'Aigle in Pfulgriesheim is a good example of the sort of simple village tavern in which this speciality can be found. From Wednesday to Sunday evening, wave after wave of *flammekuechen* are ordered by huge, happy family parties, from great-granny down to the smallest member, for not only does a *flammekueche* session make a very economical evening, but the dish somehow manages to appeal to all age groups.

Like so many of the pleasures of Alsace, *tarte flambée* boasts its own *Confrérie*, a brotherhood of enthusiasts who quail at the grisly thought of their speciality being violated with ketchup, or garnished with shellfish, or even – imagine – spread with apple slices, sweetened and served as a dessert. For a restaurant to qualify as a member of the *Confrérie de la véritable tarte flambée* therefore, the strictest criteria for both the component parts of the *tarte* and the baking thereof must be met. Only bread dough, cream and/or *fromage blanc*, bacon, onions and rapeseed oil may enter into the composition, and a wood-fired oven is essential. Although the rules do not actually specify the method of eating, it is generally agreed that the only acceptable plan of action is to cut it in four pieces, roll each one up or fold it over and eat it. Wonderful stuff, like *Winstubs*: the real Alsace.

SALADE DE CERVELAS ET GRUYERE

A typical Winstub *dish of sausages and Gruyère with tomatoes and hard-boiled eggs, in a mustardy dressing. Though often served before a* choucroute garnie, *it also makes an excellent lunch dish.*

Serves 6
salt, pepper
2 tbsp mustard
300 ml/½ pint/generous cup oil
8 tbsp vinegar
a small glass of water
or stock
a few lettuce leaves
6 *cervelas* sausages, skinned
6 tbsp finely chopped shallot
450 g/1 lb Gruyère, cut in thin strips
6 tomatoes, sliced
6 hard-boiled eggs
parsley

Whisk together the salt, pepper, mustard, oil, vinegar and water or stock to make a smooth vinaigrette.

Arrange the lettuce leaves on a large serving plate. Split the sausages in half lengthways and make deep incisions in them. Arrange them around the edge of the serving dish, sprinkle with the shallots and dress with the vinaigrette. In the middle put the Gruyère strips, also dressed with vinaigrette. Garnish the dish with sliced tomatoes, hard-boiled eggs and chopped parsley. Serve with plenty of warm crusty bread.

LEWERKNEPFLE

It would be difficult for these liver dumplings to sound (or indeed look) less appetizing, when in fact they are unusually delicious. Sometimes served as a garnish for chouc-route along with all the usual sausages, they also make an excellent supper dish with salad and can be eaten hot or cold.

Serves 4
2 shallots, finely chopped
1 clove garlic, mashed
butter
100 g/4 oz/4 slices white bread,
crusts removed
250 ml/9 fl oz/1 cup milk
250 g/9 oz liver (pig, calf or lamb)
100 g/4 oz smoked bacon, finely chopped
2 tbsp fine semolina or flour
3 eggs
plenty of chopped parsley and chervil
salt, pepper, nutmeg
grated Parmesan

Soften the shallots and garlic in a little butter without browning. Soak the bread in milk, then squeeze out the excess moisture and put the bread in the food processor with the shallots, garlic, liver, bacon, semolina or flour, eggs, herbs, salt, pepper and nutmeg. Blend till quite smooth.

Bring a large pan of salted water to just below simmering. Using wetted spoons, form *quenelles* with the mixture (which will be quite runny) and slide them into the water. Remove them to a warm dish as soon as they float to the top. Drizzle with sizzling butter and Parmesan, and serve with a green salad.

TARTELETTES FLAMBEES

At many of the top restaurants in Alsace, these tiny puff pastry flammekueche are served en amuse-gueule, to whet the appetite.

Makes about 36 mouthfuls
100 g/4 oz puff pastry
150 ml/¼ pint/⅔ cup curd (farmer's or pot)
cheese (fromage blanc)
3 tbsp cream
a pinch of salt
2 egg yolks
50 g/2 oz bacon, cut in tiny strips
1 shallot, finely chopped

Roll out the pastry very thinly and cut discs about 4 cm/1½ inches in diameter. Put them on a lightly greased heavy baking sheet.

Mix together the curd cheese, cream, salt and egg yolks and daub each disc with a little of the mixture. Scatter over the bacon and shallot and chill (or freeze) until needed.

Heat the oven to 230°C/450°F/Gas Mark 8 and bake the pastries for 10-12 minutes or until piping hot and the undersides are nicely golden.

FLAMMEKUECHE/TARTE FLAMBEE

Though your own home-made flammekueche *may never measure up to Madame Roth's of L'Aigle in Pfulgriesheim, this recipe nevertheless gives a pretty good result. A dandelion or lamb's lettuce salad with bacon (page 71) goes well.*

Serves 6-8
500 g/1 lb bread dough (e.g. *petits pains au lait,* page 35, or *pains au pavot,* page 35), or pizza dough
150 ml/¼ pint/⅔ cup double (heavy) cream
150 ml/¼ pint/⅔ cup curd (farmer's or pot) cheese (*fromage blanc*)
salt and pepper
2 tbsp oil
200 g/7 oz smoked bacon, cubed
2 medium onions, sliced thinly

Preheat the oven to maximum heat.

Allow the bread dough to rise once, knock down and then roll or pat out extremely thinly on a large heavy rectangular baking sheet (or 2 if necessary). Mix together the cream, curd cheese, salt, pepper and oil and spread it over the top.

Scatter the bacon and onions on top and bake immediately in the hot oven for about 15 minutes or until dappled with gold. They should be sizzling hot but still bendy. Cut in slices, roll or fold them up and eat with the fingers.

LES GRANDES TABLES
D'ALSACE

In the regions of France which boast the finest food, three characteristics tend to be found: a deeply-rooted gastronomic tradition, a flourishing wine trade and a goodly number of well-lined purses. With its centuries-old convention of wonderful food and warm hospitality, its outstanding wines and its post-war affluence (after the Ille de France, it is the richest region in the country), Alsace fits the bill on all counts. Not surprisingly, it claims one of the highest concentrations of Michelin stars in the whole of provincial France.

An interesting feature shared by all the top restaurants in Alsace is that however grand the food, regional touches are always reassuringly in evidence: a succulent stew of frogs' legs with crunchy *choucroute* and melting *foie gras* makes its appearance at the Auberge de l'Ill; hop shoots tasting hauntingly of asparagus come with lightly poached eggs *chez* Emile Jung at Le Crocodile in Strasbourg; at Le Cerf in Marlenheim, a favourite entrée from Robert and Michel Husser features pike-perch larded with minutely diced bacon served over a bed of shredded cabbage with a horseradish sauce; at Aux Armes de France in Ammerschwihr, chef Philippe Gaertner amuses himself playing on the familiar Alsace asparagus theme by alternating green with white and providing a variation in the form of a lightly curried, Sauternes-sweetened hollandaise sauce. The following selected restaurants magnificently represent *les grandes tables d'Alsace* beginning with Alsace's most famous gastronomic landmark, the Auberge de l'Ill (pictured opposite).

L'AUBERGE DE L'ILL

In an area not short of outstanding restaurants, the Auberge occupies a special position as a sort of honorary grandmother of the *grandes tables*, commanding a mixture of admiration, respect and affection. When Paul Haeberlin recently received the *grand Bretzel d'or* (Alsace's answer to the Oscar, awarded in recognition of outstanding efforts in many different fields on behalf of the region), one of the things that touched this great chef most was the 'guard of honour' provided by eight of his fellow chefs from Alsace. Dressed in their whites and *toques*, they had assembled to salute their *primus inter pares* and to show their approval of the panel's decision to honour him in this way.

The present inn evolved from a simple establishment called zum Grünem Baum (later L'Arbre Vert) run by Frédéric and Frédérique Haeberlin, great-grandparents of the present owners. The speciality was *matelote* (freshwater fish stew), a favourite dish of the artist Hansi. Jean-Pierre recalls with a chuckle that the Haeberlins' version was known as *la matelote protestante*, while the Mullers at La Truite across the bridge served *la matelote catholique*: a nice example of the religious tolerance and spirit of friendly rivalry which has always characterized Alsace. The Mullers still serve one of the best *matelotes* in the area, while the Haeberlins, with their superb cuisine and fabled hospitality, have developed in their own chosen direction as worldwide ambassadors for the Alsace in which they are so firmly rooted. As ever, the families are the best of friends.

During the Second World War, the village was the scene of violent combat and both the bridge and the inn were destroyed. Paul Haeberlin played his part in the First French Army as *chef de cuisine* on General de Lattre's staff, while his younger brother Jean-Pierre was of the generation conscripted into the German army: a chillingly common situation in many Alsace families in the last war.

Later demobilized from their respective units, the two brothers called a family conference to decide whether to move to proposed premises in the beautiful (and relatively unscathed) village of Riquewihr, or whether to resurrect the inn on its superb site beside the river Ill. The vote was to stay; plans were drawn up by architect Jean-Pierre and L'Auberge de l'Ill was born. It received its first star in 1952, the second in 1957, and the hat trick was completed ten years later. Since then the Haeberlins have played host to the Queen Mother and to

The Haeberlin family: Jean-Pierre, Paul and Marc (l. to r.)

Pre-prandial aperitifs in the Auberge garden

President Giscard d'Estaing, to film stars and astronauts, as well as to countless families and groups of friends gathered to celebrate some special occasion.

For Paul, the idea of pursuing any profession other than that of cook was always inconceivable, and to this day he is manifestly happier behind his *piano* (stove) than in the limelight so often thrust upon him. His son Marc increasingly shares the kitchen responsibilities, skilfully meshing creative new ideas with his father's immense experience. The huge menu, its cover illustrated by gifted watercolourist Jean-Pierre, shows the combined influences of father and son. Enshrined in the middle is a selection of dishes entitled *les spécialités qui ont fait la renommée de L'Auberge de l'Ill*, such as the souffléd salmon, and the *pêche Haeberlin*. To either side are dishes which change with the seasons and which give both father and son a freer rein. Creations which reflect their beloved Alsace balance others which draw widely on other sources for inspiration. An amusing interpretation of the famous Monday morning washday dish *Baeckeoffe* has its layers of meats and vegetables laced with truffles and comes served in a tiny, elegant casserole. The pigeon breast *en croûte* with cabbage and truffles was created by Marc on the occasion of the investiture of his father and uncle with the *Ordre National du Mérite*.

Jean-Pierre recently retired after twenty-four years' service to the community as village mayor. Apart from the regular tasks of marrying local couples and attending to village business, he was also responsible in 1967 for twinning Illhaeusern with Collonges-au-Mont d'Or, home of the Haeberlins' colleague and friend Paul Bocuse. How he also finds time to act as chief host at the Auberge is a mystery to most.

The dining room is a slightly alarming shade of green, but through the huge picture windows is the world-famous view out over the garden (where pre-prandial aperitifs are taken in the summer) to the little half-timbered cottage and the weeping willows bending low to the river. Paul's son-in-law Marco heads a dining-room team of fifteen which includes both men and women, all of them multilingual, some of them also family members, all *alsaciens*. The team spirit extends beyond the dining room and kitchen on to the football pitch, where the Auberge XI regularly strikes terror into the hearts of rival teams in the local league.

Sommelier Serge Dubs, since 1989 *Meilleur Sommelier du Monde* (World's Best Wine Waiter) seems to be a sort of honorary member of this huge clan. His encyclopaedic knowledge equips him better than most to talk of soils,

Le Meilleur Sommelier du Monde: *Serge Dubs*

yields and *grands crus*, but he is really happiest talking about (and with) people and about tasting. He baulks at the idea of naming an 'up-and-coming' Alsace grower and emphasizes the role played by the great names like Trimbach, Hugel and Beyer in establishing the reputation of Alsace fine wines.

Under pressure he will admit to a weakness for Josmeyer wines (Wintzenheim) ('one of the best vinifiers in Alsace, the thinking man's grower'), and to those of Zind-Humbrecht (*'une maison qui bouge!'* – 'a firm on the move'). He further believes that the co-operatives' wines should not be scorned, particularly Turckheim. 'A good *sommelier*', he observes finally, 'can make an excellent meal outstanding.' Certainly, with his extraordinary warmth, exceptional knowledge and total lack of pomposity, Serge Dubs adds yet another dimension to the experience of dining at the Auberge.

FEUILLETE DE PIGEONNEAU AU CHOU ET AUX TRUFFES

*Tender pigeon breasts are cloaked in bright
green leaves and a* farce, *studded with inky black
truffles and wrapped up in a puff pastry parcel.*

Serves 4
4 pigeons
salt and pepper
1 tbsp cognac
3-4 tbsp port
100 g/4 oz belly pork (fresh side pork)
100 g/4 oz boneless chicken breast
50 g/2 oz foie gras
1 shallot, finely chopped
100 g/4 oz/1 stick butter
1 egg
2 truffles, each 50 g/2 oz, peeled (keep
peelings)
vegetables for stock
herbs for stock
a Savoy cabbage (green, curly)
250 g/9 oz puff pastry
1 egg yolk

Cut the breasts from pigeons or have the butcher do
this for you. Season and marinate them for 2 hours in
the cognac and 1 tbsp port. Chop or process together
the remaining flesh, livers and hearts of the pigeons,
plus the pork, chicken and *foie gras.* Soften the shallot
in a knob of butter and add this to the stuffing with
the egg. Season with salt and pepper, beat well to
blend and lighten the stuffing. Chill.

Make a stock for the sauce with the pigeon bones,
truffle peelings, vegetables, herbs and water to cover.
After simmering gently for several hours, strain and
reduce to about a cupful.

Wash the cabbage. Reserve two large leaves, cut in
half, discard the central rib and blanch briefly in
boiling salted water. Drain, refresh in cold water, pat
dry. Cut the rest in very fine strips and sweat in a
covered pan in another knob of butter and water for
10 minutes. Tip out and allow to cool.

Roll out the pastry 3 mm/⅛ inch thick and cut into
four large rectangles. Put a cabbage leaf at one end of
each pastry piece, spread a fine layer of stuffing over
it, then press on top a layer of shredded cooked
cabbage. Lay on top slices of truffle, more stuffing, the
pigeon breast and a final thin layer of stuffing. Press it
all down gently but firmly. Wet the outside edge of
the pastry, fold the uncovered end up over everything
to make a parcel, pressing the edges together to seal.
Trim, fold the edges under and put on a greased
baking sheet. Decorate with pastry shapes made from
trimmings and glaze with egg yolk. Chill for at least
an hour before baking.

Bake at 220°C/425°F/Gas Mark 7 for 20 minutes.
Serve with a sauce based on the well-reduced pigeon
stock (made from the bones and truffle peelings)
finished with the remaining port and butter.

LA MATELOTE PROTESTANTE D'ILLHAUESERN

A simple, freshwater fish stew whose ingredients in the old days would have come straight out of the River Ill at the bottom of the Haeberlins' garden.

Serves 6
about 2 kg/4 lb assorted freshwater fish on the
bone (e.g. eel, pike, perch, tench, trout)
1 leek
1 carrot
1 onion
small bayleaf
sprig each of thyme and tarragon
small clove garlic
4 shallots, finely chopped
125 g /4½ oz/1 stick butter
1 bottle Riesling
salt and pepper
200 g/7 oz mushrooms, quartered
2-3 tbsp flour
250 ml/9 fl oz/1 cup double (heavy) cream
2 egg yolks
juice of ½ lemon, a scraping of nutmeg
1 tbsp finely chopped parsley

Skin the eel; clean and scale all the fish and cut in pieces. Keep the heads and tails to make a fish stock with the leek, carrot, onion, bayleaf, herbs and garlic and 1½ litres/2½ pints/6 cups water. Simmer for 30 minutes, strain, return to the pan and reduce to 1 litre/1½ pints/4 cups by fast boiling. Set aside.

Soften the shallots in 25 g/1 oz/2 tbsp butter. Add the Riesling and the reserved stock. Season to taste and bring to the boil. Add first the eel (which takes longest to cook), then after 5 minutes add successively the pike, tench, perch and trout. Check the seasoning and simmer for a further 10 minutes.

Sauter the mushrooms in another 25 g/1 oz/2 tbsp butter. Melt the remaining butter in a large pan and stir in enough flour to make a smooth paste. Cook for 5 minutes, then cool. Lift the fish out of the stock and keep it warm, with the mushrooms. Whisk the stock into the butter and flour, return to the heat and bring to the boil. Cook for at least 10 minutes to concentrate the flavour. Remove from the heat, whisk in the cream and egg yolks. Check the seasoning, add lemon juice and nutmeg to taste. Pour the sauce over the fish and mushrooms and sprinkle with the parsley. Serve with fresh noodles.

TARTE AU FROMAGE BLANC DE MADAME DUBS

Madame Dubs is the wife of the sommelier at the Auberge. Such is the renown of her cheesecake that faithful customers of the restaurant regularly place their order with her and bear them off home across the Rhine.

Serves 8
250 g/9 oz sweet shortcrust (basic pie) pastry
500 g/1 lb curd (farmer's or pot) cheese
(*fromage blanc*)
200 g/7 oz sugar
1 packet of vanilla sugar or 1 tsp vanilla
essence (extract)
4 eggs, separated
200 ml/7 fl oz/scant cup double (heavy) cream
100 g/4 oz/⅔ cup currants macerated in 1
tbsp kirsch or the grated zest of 1 lemon
(optional)

Matelote beside the River Ill

Roll out the pastry to fit a 30 cm/12 inch quiche tin with removable base. Bake the pastry blind.

Whisk together the cheese, half the sugar, the vanilla sugar or essence (extract), egg yolks and cream.

Beat the egg whites with the remaining sugar until stiff but not dry and fold them into the mixture. (Fold in the optional macerated currants or lemon zest.)

Heat the oven to 200°C/400°F/Gas Mark 6 and bake the tart for about half an hour or until set and lightly golden.

Remove from the oven and invert over a cake rack. Sprinkle with icing (confectioners') sugar before serving, at room temperature.

The dining room at Le Crocodile

EMILE JUNG

Writing of Le Crocodile in his 1921 guide to eating and dining in France, Curnonsky ('Prince of Gastronomes') limited himself to observing that it was possible 'to enjoy an honest meal in this popular restaurant' just off the Place Kléber in the centre of Strasbourg. Suspended over the expectant diners in those days, licking his chops in greedy anticipation of a good meal, was a huge stuffed crocodile reputed to have been brought back by a certain Captain Ackermann from the banks of the Nile to those of the Ill. In 1971, when Emile Jung took over the restaurant, the crocodile was consigned to the corridor, the style of cooking evolved from the simple to the sublime, and it was increasingly the turn of the diners to lick their lips in happy anticipation.

Recognition of Emile Jung's talents as a great chef has been building up steadily ever since, and climaxed in March 1989 when Le Crocodile became one of only nineteen three-star restaurants in France. Where before it had merited a mere detour, now – overnight – it was considered worth the journey. 'People expect me to have changed, just because of the three stars,' he comments in some bewilderment; 'I haven't changed; maybe it's just that some people *want* to see me differently.' The figure is slim, elegant (an excellent advertisement for his product); pin-striped trousers and Gucci shoes emerge from beneath the spotless whites; the face, on the other hand, is reassuringly round and jolly.

In the kitchen, he mistrusts the idea of 'creating new dishes': 'I do not create,' he says firmly, 'I extrapolate.' Fine food needs to be based on classic culinary principles from which inspired variations may then spring. Curious to know what chefs eat on their night off ('yoghurt with cinnamon', murmured his svelte wife Monique), I asked for a suggestion for Sunday supper; he volunteered a bread(crumb)ed chicken suprême

Le Crocodile

served with a sauce based on Escoffier's bortsch – and promptly disappeared upstairs to photocopy the classic recipe.

A calm, ordered man, he particularly likes the idea of creating some sort of order from the delicious chaos of a basketful of raw materials. At a 'pick-your-own' market garden on the outskirts of Strasbourg, he selects herbs, salads and vegetables (pausing to pick a few blackcurrant leaves for pastry chef Fred's celebrated *crème anglaise*), then retreats to the kitchen to make some sense out of the gorgeous disorder of colours, textures and flavours. Later, explaining the dish he has in mind, he sketches it on the nearest available piece of paper to make sure you have understood not only the ingredients, but the composition on the plate, which is of crucial importance to him.

Like all the great chefs in Alsace, he draws heavily on local ingredients, using them in sometimes unexpected combinations. Some of his dishes bear names which evoke characters from Alsace literature or gastronomy, others immortalize the name of the supplier of one of the component parts. The *terrine de volaille pistachée Fritz Kobus*, for instance, honours the hero of the Alsace classic *L'Ami Fritz*, while the inventor of *pâté de foie gras de Strasbourg*, Jean-Pierre Clause, is celebrated in the fillet of beef with *foie gras* encased in pastry. The *Père Woelffle* of *suprême de sandre Père Woelffle* fame is none

other than the supplier of the *choucroute* which is sandwiched between the fillets of pike-perch in this best-known of the chef's dishes.

The peach-coloured dining room exudes elegance, comfort and warmth. A phalanx of smiling staff moves to greet you, headed by Monique Jung (herself trained at the Strasbourg Hotel School) and ably assisted by *Maître d'hôtel* Bernard Epp and a team of accomplished waiters. Though Emile Jung combines the profession of chef with that of *sommelier*, in the dining room it is the turn of Gilbert Mestrallet to guide you through the outstanding wine list which draws on many sources. Several pages of the best Alsace names from the Haut- and Bas-Rhin categorized by grape variety, precede a classic range of Bordeaux, Burgundies and Rhônes, plus interesting selections from Germany, Italy and Spain. Mondays (ostensibly a day of rest for the staff) are set aside by Mestrallet for tastings with selected growers. For the service of Alsace wines, he has designed some extremely elegant glasses which preserve the classic Alsace shape but allow plenty of room for swirling and sniffing, with the familiar green stems (which distort the colour of the wine) replaced by plain ones. Unsurprisingly, perhaps, the wines of 'thinking man's grower' Jean Meyer (Josmeyer, Wintzenheim) hold a special appeal for philosopher-chef Jung, while those of Mochel in Traenheim in the Bas-Rhin constitute for him *un excellent souvenir*, especially when tasted (still fermenting) from the barrel last autumn.

To Emile Jung, the production of a great meal is clearly more than just an exercise in technical perfection: 'We are in the business of happiness, purveyors of pleasure, by appointment to the people!' he grins. Just how seriously he and his whole team take this business of happiness can only really be appreciated by going there and experiencing the full Crocodile treatment.

Le Chef – *Emile Jung*

GATEAUX DE FOIES BLONDS DE VOLAILLE AU COULIS DE MAIS

Palest chicken livers are mixed with three times their weight in cream and just enough eggs to set the custard lightly, turned out onto a sweetcorn coulis, served with a mushroom and tomato sauce and garnished with tiny vegetables.

Serves 6
100 g/4 oz palest chicken livers, trimmed
300 ml/½ pint/a generous cup double (heavy) cream
2 eggs
1 egg yolk
salt, pepper, nutmeg
Sauces
6 tbsp white Vermouth
200 ml/7 fl oz/scant cup Alsace Riesling
2 shallots, finely chopped
2 tomatoes, peeled and chopped
150 g/5 oz mushrooms, sliced
250 ml/9 fl oz/1 cup chicken stock
350 ml/generous half pint/1½ cups whipping cream
lemon juice
200 g/7 oz canned sweetcorn
3 tbsp single (light) cream
tiny vegetables

Liquidize the chicken livers to a smooth purée with the cream, eggs, yolk, salt, pepper and nutmeg. Strain

the mixture. Butter 6 ramekins (125 ml/¼ pint/½ cup capacity) and pour in the mixture. Bake in a bain-marie for 40 minutes in a 150°C/300°F/Gas Mark 2 oven until just firm and a skewer inserted in the middle comes out clean.

For the sauce, boil together the Vermouth, Riesling, shallots, tomatoes and mushrooms until reduced by half. Add the chicken stock and reduce again by half. Whisk in the whipping cream and simmer gently until the sauce is the consistency of thin cream. Check the seasoning and sharpen with a few drops of lemon juice.

Purée the sweetcorn in the liquidizer with the 3 tablespoons of cream, sieve and season to taste. Heat through, then pour onto warm plates, turn out the custards on top, spoon the sauce around and garnish with tiny vegetables.

Pot-au-feu d'agneau aux poivrons rouges

POT-AU-FEU D'AGNEAU AU POIVRONS ROUGES

Leaves of Swiss chard are spread with a chicken mousseline, wrapped around the lamb fillets, gently simmered and served with neatly turned pot-au-feu vegetables.

Serves 6
2 best end necks (racks) of lamb
salt and pepper
a little oil
1 carrot
1 onion
1 clove garlic
bouquet garni
1 sweet red pepper, seeded and chopped
50 g/2 oz boneless chicken breast
4 tbsp double (heavy) cream
6-8 large, fine leaves of Swiss chard
tiny spring vegetables (carrots, turnips, spring
onions (scallions), peas etc.)

Remove the bones from the lamb to give two well-trimmed fillets each weighing about 300 g/10 oz. Season the fillets and tie them with fine string. Sear them in hot oil for 2 minutes each side. Leave to cool, then remove the strings. Make a stock with the bones, salt, pepper, carrot, onion, garlic, bouquet garni, red pepper and water to cover. Simmer gently for 2-3 hours; cool, strain, degrease. Boil down hard to reduce and concentrate the flavour.

In the food processor, reduce the chicken breast to a purée, then work in the cream and salt and pepper to taste. Blanch the chard leaves; drain, refresh and pat them dry.

Lay out a generous sheet of non-PVC plastic film and arrange some of the chard leaves on top (rib side up) to cover an area about three times the size of the fillet. Pat them dry with a tea(dish)-towel, spread them finely with half the mousseline, then put a lamb fillet on top.

Roll it up tightly in the plastic film and tie the ends. Repeat the procedure with the remaining chard leaves, mousseline and lamb fillet.

Shortly before serving, drop the fillets in a pan of barely simmering water and lay a plate on top of them to stop them floating.

Cook for 25 minutes. Meanwhile cook the spring vegetables in boiling salted water until just tender. Drain and refresh them, then heat them through in some of the lamb stock.

Discard plastic film, cut each fillet carefully into 6-8 slices and serve 3-4 per person with the vegetables and a little stock.

POMMES ET RAISINS EN STREUSEL ANNELYSE

Streusel *is a sort of crumble topping found locally on sweet breads and desserts. This delightful apple and currant crumble is a development of Fred's (the pastry chef).*

Serves 8
16 prunes
½ litre/1 pint/2 cups red wine
2 lemon slices
800 g/1¾ lb Granny Smith apples, peeled and chopped
75 g/3 oz/scant ½ cup sugar
75 g/3 oz/½ cup currants
2 pinches powdered cinnamon
juice of ½ lemon
Crumble
50 g/2 oz/4 tbsp soft butter
50 g/2 oz/¼ cup sugar
50 g/2 oz/scant ½ cup plain (all-purpose) flour
50 g/2 oz/⅔ cup ground almonds

Soak the prunes overnight in warm water. Drain and bring them just to a boil in the wine with the lemon slices. Leave to one side to infuse. Cook the apples with the sugar, currants, cinnamon and lemon juice in a covered pan for barely 10 minutes.

For the crumble, rub or process together briefly the butter, sugar, flour and almonds. Sprinkle it on to a baking sheet and bake at 220°C/425°F/Gas Mark 7 for 5 minutes or until lightly golden.

Butter lightly 8 rings, each 4 cm/1½ inches high and 7.5 cm/3 inches in diameter (use 200 g/7 oz tuna cans with top and bottom removed). Put them on a baking sheet. Put a poached prune in the bottom of each one and fill three-quarters full with apples. Scatter the crumble on top and bake for 10 minutes. Lift the circles and their contents carefully with a fish slice (spatula) onto warm serving plates and remove the circles. Sprinkle each one with icing (confectioners') sugar, and around them pour a little *crème anglaise* flavoured with kirsch. Serve with a second poached prune, a selection of sorbets (apple is especially nice) and fresh fruit.

THE HUSSERS OF MARLENHEIM

It is not difficult to picture a nineteenth-century mail coach clattering down the dusty road from Strasbourg to Saverne through Marlenheim, the weary postman arrested by the warm, welcoming glow from the courtyard of Le Cerf, stabling his horses and falling gratefully in through the doors of this wonderful old inn. Though dusty horsemen are all too rare a sight in the courtyard nowadays, Le Cerf's appeal as a hospitable village inn has – thanks to the Husser family – not only been preserved, but carefully nurtured. Today it has become a sort of gastronomic staging post, a place to pause from the hectic pace of life, to enjoy superb food in the best of company.

Upon your arrival, a member of the family will be there to greet you on the doorstep. On a little table by the entrance is perched a basket of fresh herbs bound for the kitchen, enlivened by bright splashes of borage and nasturtium flowers. The dining room is panelled in light wood, the curtains are elegant but unfussy; on each table is a white porcelain plaque on which the diner's name will have been written. The food is a skilful blend of ancient Alsace and modern Husser, satisfyingly delicate, a triumphant combination of simplicity and subtlety. Upstairs from the geranium-festooned courtyard, rooms have been thoughtfully provided to which you can beat a retreat after a memorable Marlenheim meal.

The family atmosphere is one of the greatest charms of Le Cerf. Granny Husser, with her chic iron-grey hair, busies herself with the bills and the breakfasts. Her son Robert, who nursed the restaurant from one- to two-star status, is most often to be found behind the swing doors, where the steady gaze over his half-moon spectacles seldom misses a trick. After the heat and bustle of the kitchen, he takes refuge in the cool of the kitchen garden, source of herbs, vegetables, salads and great satisfaction to this plainly contented man. Taking an

Robert Husser, contented gardener-chef

increasing share of the kitchen responsibilities is his son Michel, Senderens-trained but steadily developing his own unmistakable style. In the dining room are two more generations of Husser wives: Marcelle and Cathy, married respectively to Robert and Michel. The fourth generation, Clara and Melina, skip in and out of the kitchen and keep the *brigade* on their toes; each has a dish named after her. Of all the *grandes tables* of Alsace, Le Cerf strikes me as the most unfailingly warm and unceremonious, a uniquely successful combination of a 'familiar' atmosphere – in the best sense of the word – with thoroughgoing professionalism. Little wonder that stage coaches have come to a halt so regularly outside its doors for so many years.

Though Robert trained at the hotel school in Strasbourg, he describes himself as a self-taught cook (*un autodidacte*), greatly inspired by (and indebted to) his

Courtyard at Le Cerf, Marlenheim

grandfather, who took over the inn in 1930. Michel admits to having been hugely influenced by the creative genius of Alain Senderens, with whom he worked during the early Archestrate days. But both father and son agree that the biggest shift in emphasis in the Husser style of cooking dates from the day the kitchen garden came into its own. Fellow gardeners will readily identify with Robert's observation that 'cooking with your own lovingly grown herbs and vegetables is an affair of the heart.' The result – *'une cuisine de sensibilité'* – is a sensitive reinterpretation of Alsace cuisine, a game of seemingly familiar themes with intriguing variations, closely attuned to the seasons.

In the depths of winter you might find a salad of minutely diced brawn (head cheese) set over a mound of lentils and lamb's lettuce and warmly dressed with horseradish, a dish created in honour of *le grand-père Wagner*. Spring brings asparagus fever to Alsace, and *chez* Husser the spears arrange themselves around delicate sweetbread raviolis, with wild mushrooms to complete the picture. Twice a week, instead of the stagecoach from Strasbourg, a van from Brittany delivers its load of fresh fish and shellfish. Summer brings salads of Breton lobster with *foie gras* and basil, or red mullet with sherry vinegar and little finger-sized courgettes (zucchini) from the garden. (Beware if you plan a visit to Marlenheim around 15 August: every year at this time, borrowing rather freely from the classic Alsace novel *L'Ami Fritz*, the village stages a re-enactment of the marriage of the hardened old bachelor Fritz Kobus to his beloved Sûzel; in all the hotels and restaurants it's standing room only.)

Though the roebuck season opens as early as June in Alsace, it is in the autumn that Le Cerf (as you might expect of an inn under the sign of the stag) serves its most stunning selection of game: wild duck, partridge,

The Husser family

venison and pheasant, each beautifully cooked and imaginatively garnished: sweetcorn fritters for the partridge, little parcels of *choucroute* for the pheasant, gnocchi for the wild duck; and with the venison the almost inevitable *spätzle* (p56), satisfying little squiggles of pasta without which no game dish in this part of the world is considered complete.

Desserts are simply spectacular, served on huge, icing sugar-bordered plates. Most have to be ordered in advance, and make considerable play of sweet-sharp, warm-cold contrasts. Home-made ices are original and delicious: a light, sharp version made of curd cheese goes with the cherry crêpes; a fragrant *miel de sapin* (pine honey) counterbalances the hot *quetsch* plum dessert; cinnamon ice is served with the *mirabelle* or apple tarts.

Le Cerf's wine list includes all the great names, but for advice on young, up-and-coming growers, especially in the Bas-Rhin, consult the young *sommelier* David Kaminski. Recent winner of the *Meilleur Jeune Sommelier de France* trophy, his infectious enthusiasm for his subject matches his impressive understanding of the diner's needs.

'The old stag'

VELOUTE FROID A L'OSEILLE
AUX QUENELLES DE SAUMON

A delectable spring starter: pale pink ovals of chopped smoked salmon floated over an icy green sorrel soup with a crunchy contrast of croûtons and finely chopped salad vegetables.

Serves 6
150 g/5 oz sorrel
200 ml/7 fl oz/scant cup chicken stock
50 g/2 oz potatoes, boiled and peeled
½ litre/1 pint/2 cups whipping cream
salt and pepper
150 g/5 oz smoked salmon
½ cucumber
1 small bunch radishes, trimmed
1 tbsp whipped cream
chervil
croûtons

Wash and strip the sorrel of central ribs. Purée in the liquidizer with the stock and potato. Blend in the cream, season to taste and chill.

Chop the salmon, cucumber and radish in very tiny cubes. Mix half the vegetables with the salmon cubes and bind with the tablespoon of whipped cream. Shape into ovals (4 per person) and chill.

Just before serving, divide the soup between 6 chilled soup plates. Put 4 salmon ovals in each plate, sprinkle on the remaining chopped vegetables and garnish with sprigs of chervil and croûtons tossed in butter at the last minute.

RAVIOLES DE RIS DE VEAU AUX ASPERGES ET AUX CHAMPIGNONS SAUVAGES

Diced sweetbreads and foie gras *are enclosed in superfine pasta and garnished with green asparagus spears and wild mushrooms; a ravishing dish with interesting contrasts of colour, texture and flavour.*

Serves 6
600 g/1¼ lb sweetbreads
flour
salt and pepper
165 g/5½ oz/11 tbsp butter
2 shallots, finely chopped
100 g/4 oz slice raw duck *foie gras*, cubed
chervil, parsley, chives
2 tbsp double (heavy) cream
2 egg yolks
250 g/9 oz pasta dough (page 136)
200 g/7 oz wild mushrooms (e.g. chanterelles, morels, pleurotus, boletus etc.)
300 ml/½ pint/generous cup chicken stock
24 green asparagus
1 chicken stock (bouillon) cube
chervil sprigs

Soak the sweetbreads in cold water for 1 hour. Blanch in boiling salted water, drain and refresh in cold water. Separate into little nodules, strip away all membrane and nerves, toss in seasoned flour and fry briskly in a little butter to colour lightly. Remove them to a bowl. In the same pan, stew most of the shallots (keep some back for cooking with the mushrooms) without allowing them to colour. Add them to the bowl with the *foie gras*, finely chopped herbs, cream and egg yolks to bind.

Roll out half the pasta dough as finely as possible with a rolling pin or pasta machine. Place teaspoons of filling at regular intervals all over the pasta. Brush the spaces between mounds of filling with water. Roll out the remaining dough and press it on top. Cut out ravioli. Leave them to dry out on a lightly floured tea (dish)-towel set over a cake rack.

Wash the mushrooms and cook them with the reserved chopped shallot in the stock. Lift them out with a slotted spoon and reduce the stock by half. Off the heat, whisk in the remaining butter in small pieces.

Cook the asparagus in boiling salted water until just tender (about 12 minutes). Dissolve the stock cube in a large pan of boiling water and simmer the ravioli in it until just tender (about 3 minutes). Fish one out and taste the edge of the pasta to be sure. Arrange them on hot plates with the asparagus spears, interspersed with the mushrooms. Garnish with chervil sprigs.

ROGNONNADE DE VEAU A L'ACHE DE MONTAGNE A LA CREME D'ECHALOTE

*Slices of veal are beaten out flat, scattered
with leaves of lovage and wrapped around
a strip of veal kidney. Serve with spinach and
spätzle (page 56).*

Serves 6
300 g/10 oz veal fillet (boneless round)
salt and pepper
several leaves of lovage or celery
1 veal kidney
200 g/7 oz shallots, finely chopped
butter
300 ml/½ pint/generous cup Riesling or other
dry white wine
3 tbsp sherry vinegar
6 tbsp veal stock
2 tbsp double (heavy) cream

Cut the veal into 50 g/2 oz escalopes (scallops) and
beat them out about 2-3 mm/⅛ inch thick. Season.
Lay three or four lovage or celery leaves on each one.
Cut the veal kidney lengthwise into 6 long strips of
equal size. Remove the central core carefully. Roll up
the kidney strips in the escalopes, secure with
toothpicks.

Soften the shallots in butter, moisten with the wine
and vinegar, reduce almost to nothing, then whisk in
the veal stock and cream. Bubble up briefly, then tip
into the liquidizer and blend until quite smooth.
Check the seasoning.

Sear the paupiettes in hot butter on all sides until
golden. Finish the cooking in a 200°C/400°F/Gas
Mark 6 oven for 10 minutes. Remove the toothpicks,
cut each paupiette into 4-5 slices, arrange around hot
plates with a bed of spinach in the middle and the
spätzle round about.

AUMONIERES AUX GRIOTTES, COULIS DE FRAMBOISE ET GLACE AU FROMAGE BLANC

An aumonière *is a begging bag, filled here
with kirsch-soaked cherries, cream and
custard, baked in the oven, set over a sharp
raspberry sauce and served with a light curd
cheese ice cream.*

Serves 6
12 thin crêpes (page 156)
500 g/1 lb raspberries
icing (confectioner's) sugar to taste
500 g/1 lb curd (farmer's or pot) cheese
(*fromage blanc*)
35 g/1½ oz/3 tbsp sugar
6 tbsp *crème anglaise*
400 g/14 oz Morello cherries preserved in
kirsch
2 tbsp chopped praline
6 tbsp *crème pâtissière*
3 tbsp whipped cream
melted butter

Fold the crêpes in four and cut a ½-cm/¼-inch
ribbon off the outside edge to make the begging bag
strings. Purée the raspberries with icing (confectioners') sugar to taste and push through a sieve to
eliminate pips.

Whisk together the curd cheese, sugar and *crème*

anglaise. Freeze in a *sorbetière* (or in the freezer, stirring up regularly to prevent ice crystals forming).

Mix together the cherries, praline, *crème pâtissière* and whipped cream and fill the crêpes with the mixture. Tie the neck of the begging bags with the reserved crêpe ribbons. About 15 minutes before serving, heat the oven to 150°C/300°F/Gas Mark 2.

Brush the bags with melted butter, sprinkle with icing (confectioners') sugar and bake in the preheated oven for 10-12 minutes.

Use large white plates if possible and sprinkle the border with icing (confectioners') sugar. Pour a little raspberry coulis onto each plate, and serve two aumonières with two ovals of ice cream.

Rognonnade de veau à l'âche de montagne

CHEZ GAERTNER, AMMERSCHWIHR

'I shall not quickly forget my first dinner at Gaertner's', wrote Elizabeth David in *French Provincial Cooking*, in 1960. She was not the first person to find dining at Aux Armes de France an unforgettable experience and many more have since taken away their own store of memories of this warm and wonderful house.

Pierre Gaertner's mother established the name of the restaurant in the twenties with such simple and delicious fare as poached sausages with warm horseradish sauce and creamy apple tarts. A battered old copy of the Michelin guide brought in recently by a customer showed that in 1938 they had already been singled out with one star as a good table in their category. Then came the war, in which Ammerschwihr paid a particularly heavy price; caught in the crossfire between the Allied (mainly American) and German forces in the battle for the strategic *poche de Colmar* in December 1944, eighty-five per cent of this once-beautiful medieval and renaissance village was reduced to rubble.

As Ammerschwihr rose, phoenix-like, from the ashes, so also Aux Armes de France, rebuilt in 1950, began its rise to fame and excellence under the guiding hand of

Pierre Gaertner. The second star quickly followed in 1953, along with a reputation for sumptuous food, true to the *terroir*. In 1986 Monsieur Gaertner was forced through illness to retire, but the succession was already assured in the shape of his two sons Philippe (head chef) and François (pastry chef). Philippe's wife Simone (whom he refers to as his ambassadress) exactly personifies the character of the house: warm, smiling, approachable, solicitous to the diner's every need.

The calm, unhurried atmosphere which is so evident in the dining room is mirrored backstage. Philippe moves quietly around the kitchen, dipping a spoon into a sauce, sniffing a sole to check for absolute freshness; bestowing here a pat on the shoulder for a job well done, exchanging there a joke, usually in the Alsace dialect. A brother-in-law appears at the back door with a catch of fresh trout: *truite au bleu* is decided upon for the family's lunch, taken at eleven o'clock, before the customer onslaught begins.

François, like many pastry chefs, is something of a solitary soul, beavering away in the cool quiet of his pastry kitchen on creations which he admits are influenced by his training *chez* Guérard, and his time spent with *chocolatiers* Christian and Bernachon. His holidays are spent far away from *haute cuisine*, camping among the Scottish lochs, feasting on chanterelles picked from under the noses of the disbelieving Scots and stewed up over the camp fire.

Philippe's food embodies – in true Gaertner style – all the flavours and fragrances of Alsace, coupled with a sureness and lightness of touch which testify to his formative years *chez* Boyer and Bocuse. Many of his sauces for fish are hollandaise-based, given flavour and character by sternly reduced stocks, and a satisfying illusion of lightness by whipped cream; meat sauces are *jus*, minimally mounted with butter.

Philippe and François Gaertner

The dining room at Aux Armes de France

On the dessert front, the *vacherin glacé* which left Elizabeth David temporarily speechless has given way to a lighter, more elegant version (see recipe p. 124). Other creations show a skilful balance of traditional and contemporary, from Alsace and elsewhere. The waffles *à l'ancienne* with a deliciously spotty vanilla ice and the *soufflé glacé à l'aspérule odorante* (a rare *eau de vie* made from woodruff) show clear signs of their Alsace pedigree.

The tall, slightly stern *maître d'hôtel* Claude Groell will soon unbend when he discovers that you are interested in his exceptionally fine wine list: as you might expect in a top restaurant buried in the heart of the best vineyards in Alsace, it is richly furnished with every kind of treasure. The house aperitif (Crémant d'Alsace with a dash of elderberry liqueur) is curious; my personal preference goes rather to Muscat, that most unbeatable of Alsace appetite-whetters, pure grapes in the glass and not a trace of sweetness.

The first-floor dining room is clad in warm wooden panelling, the tables are nicely spaced between three rooms. Big bunches of flowers adorn the tables and all around there are contented sighings. Nowadays by far the greatest number of visitors are from Germany; each year an American liberator returns to dine *chez* Gaertner and to renew his own memories. One diner was overheard to exclaim contentedly: '*Ça fait du bien!*' With its warm welcome, superb cuisine, unruffled, unhurried atmosphere, Gaertner's definitely does you good.

La dodine de lapereau

A simple, delicious and refreshing dish for summer; pieces of rabbit are layered in a terrine with finely chopped vegetables and herbs, and moistened with stock and wine which turns into a lightly set jelly when cold.

Serves 6-8
1 rabbit (about 1.5 kg/3 lb)
1 tbsp olive oil
a large bunch (125 g/4½ oz) parsley, finely chopped
small bunch chervil, finely chopped
1 tbsp chopped chives
1 tbsp chopped tarragon
1 sprig thyme
1 bayleaf
1 clove
2 cloves garlic
1 onion, finely chopped
6 small tomatoes, peeled and chopped
salt, pepper
150 ml/¼ pint/⅔ cup chicken stock
about 150 ml/¼ pint/⅔ cup dry white wine
4 sheets gelatine (or 2 tsp powdered unflavoured gelatine)
3 tbsp kirsch

Chop the rabbit into 75 g/3 oz pieces. Brush the inside of a 1.2 kg/2½ lb terrine with the olive oil. Mix

together all the prepared herbs, spices, garlic and onion and put a layer in the bottom of the terrine. Follow with some chopped tomatoes, then pieces of rabbit. Continue with the layers until everything is used up. Season the layers carefully (and rather highly) as you go. Add the chicken stock and enough wine to come up to the top of the terrine. Bake in a bain-marie at 150°C/300°F/Gas Mark 2 for 1½ hours.

Soak the sheet gelatine in cold water until floppy. (Alternatively, sprinkle powdered gelatine on to 3 tbsp cold water until spongy.) Dissolve either sort in the kirsch and pour it into the terrine. Return it to the oven for a further 15 minutes.

Leave to cool for at least 24 hours. Serve with a lentil salad and arrange oakleaf and other salad leaves decoratively around.

GATEAU DE GAMBAS AU RIWELE

*Riwele, a sort of pasta resembling short lengths
of spaghetti (which can be used instead),
are often used in Alsace as a
thickening for soups. Philippe Gaertner
whisks them into the sauce for his prawn
parcels to add a bit of texture and local colour.
Brik leaves (like superfine crêpes) can be
found in middle eastern or Moroccan shops.*

Serves 4
20 giant prawns (shrimp), raw
salt and pepper
100 g/4 oz/1 stick butter (plus extra melted for
pastry)
8 mushrooms, finely chopped
4 leaves brik pastry
2 cooked artichoke hearts, cubed
250 ml/scant ½ pint/1 cup chicken stock
1 tbsp spaghetti broken in tiny pieces
4 tbsp finely chopped parsley

Behead the prawns (shrimp), remove shells and split
them open, butterfly-style. Season and fry them
briskly for 2-3 minutes in a little butter. Remove them
and add the mushrooms. Cover and cook gently to
allow the juices to render; uncover and cook hard to
evaporate the juices.

Brush the brik pastry leaves with melted butter and
divide the prawns, mushrooms and artichoke hearts
equally between them. Fold them over into a nice
parcel and set them aside if not to be cooked
immediately. Fry them (seam sides under) in a little
hot butter in a large pan which will go into the oven.
Finish them off in a hot oven (200°C/425°F/Gas
Mark 7) for 5-6 minutes more.

Bring the stock to the boil and add the broken
spaghetti. Cook hard until reduced by half. Off the
heat whisk in the remaining butter and parsley. Pour
the sauce around the parcels.

LASAGNE DE POUSSINS AUX PETITS LEGUMES

Individual lasagne are made from fine pasta dough layered with lightly roasted chopped baby chicken and mushrooms, and served with tiny spring vegetables. Fiddly but fun, and most of it can be done in advance.

Serves 6

200 g/7 oz/1⅓ cups plain
(all-purpose) flour
salt and pepper
2 eggs
water or oil
3 poussins (squab chickens)
2 shallots, finely chopped
75 g/3 oz/6 tbsp butter
250 g/9 oz mushrooms, sliced
300 ml/½ pint/generous cup chicken stock
a selection of spring vegetables: onions,
baby carrots, leeks, broccoli and turnips
2 tbsp white Vermouth
thyme flowers or sprigs

Make up pasta dough with the flour, salt and eggs. Add a little water or oil if necessary to make a smooth, supple dough which does not stick to your hands. Rest the dough.

Roast the chickens in a 220°C/425°F/Gas Mark 7 for 10 minutes until barely cooked. Remove from the oven and take all the meat off the bones. Chop finely and tip into a bowl. (Use the bones to make stock if you wish.)

Fry the shallots in a little hot butter until golden, then add the mushrooms, salt and pepper. Cover and cook gently till the juices render, then uncover, raise the heat and cook until dry. Scrape into the bowl with the chicken and mix well.

Roll out the pasta dough as finely as you can (to a rectangle at least 70 × 50 cm/20 × 30 inches). Using a scone (biscuit)-cutter or similar instrument, cut 24 8-cm/3¼-inch discs of pasta. Bring a large pan of salted water to the boil and blanch the pieces of pasta a few at a time. Drain them. If not to be used immediately, leave them in cold water.

To assemble the lasagne, pat the pasta dry and sandwich 3 layers of chicken mixture between 4 discs of pasta. Place them in a lightly buttered ovenproof dish and moisten with 4 tablespoons stock. Cover with foil and bake in a 200°C/400°F/Gas Mark 6 oven for 15 minutes or until thoroughly hot (stick a skewer in the middle and hold it against your cheek; it should feel uncomfortably warm).

Cook the vegetables until just tender. For the sauce, reduce the remaining stock and Vermouth by half. Whisk in the remaining butter. Pour a little sauce around each lasagne and arrange the vegetables and thyme sprigs or flowers around.

VACHERINS GLACES AUX FRUITS

Individual meringue baskets are filled with real vanilla ice cream, topped with raspberry sorbet and served on a pool of red fruit sauce spiked with eau de vie de framboise.

Serves 8
4 egg whites
a pinch of salt
350 g/12 oz/1⅔ cups caster
(superfine) sugar
1 tsp vinegar
vanilla ice cream
500 g/1 lb soft red fruit (raspberries,
strawberries, redcurrants etc.)
2 tbsp *eau de vie de framboise*
raspberry sorbet
toasted slivered almonds
whipped cream (optional)

Whisk the whites with the salt until stiff but not dry. Pour on 200 g/7 oz/1 cup sugar, sprinkle on the vinegar and continue whisking until quite firm and glossy. Draw 8 6-cm/2½-inch discs on a sheet of non-stick baking (parchment) paper. Spread a layer of meringue inside each circle to make the bases; using a 1 cm/½ inch nozzle, pipe 4 rings around the circumference to make the walls. Bake in a 120°C/250°F/ Gas Mark ½ oven for 1 hour or until they no longer stick to the paper. Allow them to cool, then pack with vanilla ice cream and put them in the freezer.

Liquidize together the fruit, remaining sugar and *eau de vie* for the coulis. Push it through a sieve to eliminate pips.

Just before serving, pour a little coulis on to each plate; on top put a vacherin crowned with an oval of raspberry sorbet. Sprinkle with slivered toasted almonds. Whipped cream may also be served separately.

Vacherin glacé with sorbet and fresh fruit

CO-OPERATIVE EXCELLENCE IN THE VINEYARDS

In many wine-growing countries, the word co-operative spells mediocrity, if not downright disaster. In Alsace, however, contrary to the more usual practice of creaming off all the goodies and using the co-operative as a convenient dustbin for the rest, members contract to sell *their entire crop*, for better or for worse, to the co-operative to which they belong. Hugh Johnson acknowledges that the area has 'one of the strongest co-operative movements' whose standards 'are extremely high and [who] often provide the best bargains in the region.'

Their strength is not in question; indeed some people (notably the private growers) consider that the co-operatives have altogether too much muscle – ten per cent of all the wines produced in Alsace are made by Eguisheim's *cave*, and the combined output of all the co-operatives now matches that of the merchant growers. Mutterings of megalomania and political rumblings need not concern the consumer, however, and co-operative wines can provide an excellent introduction to the taste of Alsace, offering good sound drinking at reasonable prices.

The Pfaffenheim *cave* was nominated wine-maker of the year by the Gault-Millau magazine in 1988, and their range is worth investigation; Bennwihr's, created like so many of them just after the Second World War, produces a remarkable Gewurztraminer from the Marckrain vineyard; Ingersheim, Kientzheim and Ribeauvillé all make creditable wines which score well in comparative

tastings. Eguisheim (under the Wolfberger brand name) makes a delicious Pinot Blanc which has long been a favourite of ours.

But the name which comes most readily to people's lips in the co-operative context is that of Turckheim. I once heard its director, Jean-Paul Ritzenthaler, described as the Emile Peynaud of Alsace. A delightfully modest man, stocky, bespectacled, with a typically *alsacien* line in self-deprecating humour, Monsieur Ritzenthaler gave his charming smile and responded that this was nonetheless '*un tout petit peu exageré*!'

It may indeed be a small exaggeration to compare him with the famous Peynaud of Bordeaux, but the fact remains that as you travel around Alsace, almost whoever you talk to in the wine world, whether *sommelier*, wine merchant, fellow co-operator or – most telling of all – private grower, a striking consensus emerges: Turckheim is something special. Probably the supreme compliment came from a member of the *Grandes Maisons d'Alsace* (see page 140) – an association not notoriously lavish in its praise of co-operatives: 'There's Turckheim – and there's the rest.'

Monsieur Ritzenthaler is clear about the reasons for their particular reputation for excellence. Both he and his oenologist Monsieur Meyer have always stressed the importance of distinguishing each part of their collective 'vineyard'. On the first day of the harvest in 1988, I watched as each load of grapes was weighed as it came in, its quality registered, and the member paid accordingly, with a premium of up to thirty per cent on the best grapes from prime sites. Then each lot of grapes was set aside to be vinified with its peer. The importance of the *terroir*, the nature of the soil on which the grapes of each of their 280 members are grown, is thus paramount. 'I doubt', he said with a certain pride, 'if you will find many wine-makers drawing such fine distinctions.'

Monsieur Ritzenthaler – as a past President of the *commission des grands crus* – has played a crucial role in the shaping of the legislation governing this upper category of Alsace wines. In 1975 the first twenty-five *grands crus* were designated, followed by a further batch in 1983. All are vineyards of ancient renown, geographically and geologically homogenous, in which only the noble grapes (Riesling, Pinot Gris, Gewurztraminer and Muscat) may be grown; yields are lower than for ordinary Alsace wines. The choice of vineyards to be nominated as *grands crus* has caused bitter controversy, as has the use of vineyard names on labels. Monsieur Ritzenthaler's involvement in this contentious exercise has clearly given him some satisfaction, many headaches and plenty of insights into human nature.

One of the biggest problems of any area which aims to produce wines of quality is to persuade its growers to reduce their yields. He told me of a member of the co-operative who had tried to slip some Gewurztraminer grapes from an over-prolific site into a load from a less well-endowed one. I expressed what I hoped was the proper degree of shock-horror. 'Madame,' he remonstrated gently, 'you must understand that for this man, who lived through the war years and has built up his vines again from nothing, it is a sin, a criminal waste, to throw away what seem to him to be perfectly good grapes. By his standards, he was not being dishonest; it is simply my job to convince him of the arguments for different standards – quality over quantity.

On the question of the future of Alsace's different grape varieties, Monsieur Ritzenthaler sees good prospects for 'the three Pinots': Pinot Blanc, an ideal everyday drinking wine with good acidity and plenty of fruit; Pinot Gris, a rich, opulent wine ideal for richly sauced dishes, and a keenly priced alternative to white burgundy; and Pinot Noir, the classic grape of Burgundy, which produces in Alsace (with some notable exceptions) rosé or light red wines admirable for lunchtime drinking. All three enjoy the undeniable advantage of being easy for foreigners to pronounce, while

The picturesque village of Turckheim

sounding unmistakably French. Riesling will always have its place as the greatest wine Alsace can produce, the biggest challenge to the wine-maker, the greatest prize for the wine connoisseur. Likewise, he sees a good future for Gewurztraminer, because its appeal (to those who like heady, spicy wines) is so instant and uncomplicated. Regrettably, he foresees a decline in production of the delicate, fruity Muscat. It is a fussy grape, difficult to vinify well, and people have difficulty in placing it within a meal, when its real role is as a mouth-filling, fruit-packed, bone-dry aperitif. The often overly acidic Sylvaner will probably not be mourned by many; Chasselas, already undetectable on labels and used only in the Edelzwicker blend, may fade even further from the scene.

Finally, after all the talk about grape varieties, yields and *grands crus*, Monsieur Ritzenthaler points out that the most important thing is to look behind the bottles at the people who make the wine: '*cherchez l'homme!*'. The best sites, a wonderful summer, several square miles of stainless steel, the latest bottling plant and a series of fancy labels will all be to no avail if the wine-maker is unable, through lack of skill, to coax from his grapes their full, marvellous potential for fine wine.

In a few years' time Monsieur Ritzenthaler retires. The good news is that, like all the best leaders, he has been carefully grooming a successor. Rumour has it that the exceptional route which Turckheim has chosen to follow will not change significantly.

MATELOTE DE POISSONS DE MER AU GEWURZTRAMINER

This variation of the classic Alsace fish stew comes from Albert Worreth of L'Auberge du Jura in Kiffis: all the fish are filleted, then baked in the Gewurztraminer which later finds its way into the delectable sauce.

Serves 6
75 g/3 oz smoked bacon, cut in matchstick strips
400 g/14 oz leeks, cut in matchstick strips
1.2 kg/2½ lb fish fillets (sea bass, red mullet, sole, monkfish, salmon etc.)
salt and pepper
12 raw langoustines or large prawns (shrimp)
3 shallots, finely chopped
4 glasses Gewurztraminer
400 ml/¾ pint/1¾ cups whipping cream
50 g/2 oz/4 tbsp soft butter

In a large heavy pan, stew the bacon pieces gently until they render a little fat. Add the leeks, cover and cook for 5-6 minutes or until the juices run and the bacon pieces are just tender. Lift them out and keep them warm. Reserve the juices in the pan for the sauce.

Butter lightly a large ovenproof dish in which all the fish will fit in one layer. Season the fish pieces and put them and the langoustines in the dish. Sprinkle on the shallots and moisten with the wine.

Bake in a 200°C/400°F/Gas Mark 6 oven for 8-10 minutes or until just opaque and barely cooked. Lift them out and keep them warm with the leeks and bacon.

Tip any cooking juices from the fish and the leeks into a small pan and boil hard to reduce by half. Whisk in the cream, season carefully, then whisk in the butter.

Arrange the leeks and bacon in a little mound on each hot plate; arrange fish and langoustines around. Spoon over the sauce. Serve at once, with fresh pasta (page 136) and a good Gewurztraminer.

BOEUF GROS SEL A L'ALSACIENNE

In the rest of France, boiled beef is served with soggy vegetables; in Alsace it is altogether a more colourful and powerful dish (a favourite of Monsieur Ritzenthaler's) with its array of crunchy salads and the regulation hot horseradish sauce (l'indispensable raifort). Recipe from Monsieur Hildebrand of La Taverne du Vigneron in Guebwiller.

Serves 4
1 kg/2 lb boneless boiling beef in one piece (shoulder, silverside, bladebone, chuck etc.)
2 onions
3 carrots
2 cabbage leaves
1 leek
1 stick celery with leaves
2 bayleaves
salt and pepper
Horseradish sauce
250 g/9 oz horseradish root
a pinch of sugar
1 slice white bread soaked in milk
250 ml/9 fl oz/1 cup double (heavy) cream

Salads
4 carrots, grated
4 small beetroot (beets), cooked and
peeled, grated
1 cucumber, sliced, salted and drained
1 celeriac, peeled and grated
4 tomatoes, sliced
½ red cabbage, cooked and shredded finely
plenty of vinaigrette
4 hard-boiled eggs, chopped
gherkins
coarse salt

Put the beef in a large pot and add the vegetables, herbs, salt and pepper and water to cover. Bring gently to the boil, skimming frequently. Simmer gently for about 1½ hours or until the meat is quite tender.

Lift out the meat and keep it warm. Set aside about 1 cup of stock for the hot horseradish sauce (the rest can be served as a first course, or kept for some other use); peel and grate the horseradish and put it in a small pan with the stock and sugar. Squeeze out the bread and add it to the pan. Stir in the cream and bring just to the boil.

Slice the meat and arrange it on a serving dish. Sprinkle it with coarse salt. Around the meat arrange the salads (*en nid de cigogne*, specifies Monsieur Hildebrand: like storks' nests), each dressed with vinaigrette, and the gherkins. Serve the hot horse-radish sauce separately.

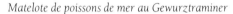
Matelote de poissons de mer au Gewurztraminer

MADAME FALLER ET SES FILLES

For some reason which I have never really understood, but for which I never cease to give thanks, the bus-loads of summer visitors to Alsace thunder past the turning to Kaysersberg and come to rest in other well-known towns and villages.

A former member of the *Décapole* (a medieval grouping of ten cities pledged to mutual assistance), Kaysersberg – its name meaning 'mountain of the Emperor' – was a significant settlement even in Roman times. It marks the transition from vineyard slopes to Vosges foothills and it dominates the entrance to the Weiss valley leading up to the Col du Bonhomme. The strategic importance of this famous pass was as well understood by the Roman armies as by the Allied troops at the end of the Second World War, and over the centuries Kaysersberg has seen many bitter conflicts. All the more appropriate therefore that the Nobel Peace Prize winner Albert Schweitzer should have been born here; in his memory the town is twinned with Lambarene in Gabon, and houses a museum devoted to his life and work.

From lunchtime in summer, the centre of Kaysersberg becomes a pedestrian precinct and you can wander up and down the main street lined with medieval half-timbered houses undisturbed by twentieth-century traffic. As you cross the beautiful sixteenth-century fortified bridge which spans the River Weiss, spare a thought for one Jean Ittel, without whose timely and courageous intervention the bridge would have been blown up by the Germans in December 1944. In the town centre, look

The house by the bridge. Previous page: *Evening sunlight on Kaysersberg*

out for the Pâtisserie Loeckel, one of the few bakers to stock regularly the elusive *kugelhopf au lard* (see page 36); all around are opportunities to taste wine and *eaux de vie*. An inscription on the town well warns against the dangers of over-indulgence in water which 'chills the stomach'. Better by far to drink in moderation 'old and subtle wine'. On the edge of the town is the Clos des Capucins, formerly a Capuchin monastery, now home of Madame Faller *et ses filles*, famous the world over for the elegance and subtlety of their wines.

To Madame Faller I owe my first tasting of memorably wonderful Rieslings. Armed with an introduction and equipped with a wine merchant brother, we arrived on what must have been one of the nastiest days of the century at this beautiful walled property set in twenty-three hectares (fifty-seven acres) of vines. My attitude towards Riesling had always been ambivalent. I was puzzled at my inability to understand why, of all the Alsace wines, it is the one of which growers are invariably proudest, but which I invariably found hardest to love. Vague murmurings by wine buffs about *le goût de pétrole* (the taste of petrol) did little to stimulate my enthusiasm.

With the first taste of 1986 Cuvée Théo (named after

Madame's late husband), it was clear that anything I had sampled in the past had been a pale and usually rather acidic imitation of the real thing. Here were fruit, flowers, honey – even pineapples. Other *cuvées* and other vintages followed, each more wonderful than the last, climaxing in an unforgettable, late-harvested, 'nobly rotted' treasure. And nowhere a trace of petrol.

I expressed my relief. Madame Faller was much amused and explained that if this is present at all, it is only in old Rieslings grown on certain soils – and then chuckled delightedly at the recollection of her own first experience of this phenomenon, when she was still something of a novice at blind tastings. So appalled was she by the first sniff that she announced to the assembled – and astonished – company that 'the grower must have had his wine vat next-door to the boiler'! It was rather heartening to imagine Madame Faller as having ever been a novice at wine tasting.

Though famous for its Rieslings, the Domaine Weinbach is probably as well or better known for its Muscats, Gewurztraminers and Pinot Gris. The latter grape, originally known in Alsace as Tokay, was first mentioned in a description of the Domaine in 1750, and was traditionally supposed to have been brought back from Hungary to Kaysersberg by Lazare de Schwendi, a sixteenth-century imperial general. It makes a colourful but confusing story, since the grape in question is clearly no relation of the Hungarian Tokay, a fact which both Hungarians and *alsaciens* are anxious to underline – hence the recent disappearance from labels of the misleading 'Tokay' prefix. Madame Faller's Pinot Noir is deeper in colour and more complex in flavour than many in the region, satisfyingly fruity, but true to the *terroir*. She dislikes the practice of some growers who try to ape a Burgundy by ageing their Pinot in small wooden barrels, asserting that '*il faut être fier de ce qu'on a*' – 'one should be proud of what one has'. Typically, she is not one to dismiss Sylvaner, an often excessively acidic grape

Madame Faller et sa fille

which is fast ceding ground to the flowery Pinot Blanc.

She talks (and writes) touchingly and frankly of her late husband Théo, a legendary figure who bestrode the narrow Alsace vineyard like something of a Colossus, and one of whose many projects was the charming Musée du vignoble et des vins d'Alsace in nearby Kientzheim. His absence is still keenly felt. After the first shock of widowhood, nine years ago, she decided that to crumple under the strain was no way in which to honour his memory. '*L'amour-propre*', she comments drily, 'is a great spur to achievement.' Was it hard for her, a woman in what is often considered a man's world? On the contrary, she responds with a great twinkle, she feels it worked to her advantage. Seeing her now, listening to her talk animatedly of the beauty and harmony of her wines, which combine the enviable attributes of immediate accessibility and great ageing potential, this is not difficult to believe.

TARTE A L'OIGNON

Classic Alsace, to be found in homes and country inns everywhere. Though some recipes include Béchamel in the filling, Madame Faller prefers to use cream. Her mother (who supervised the preparation of the one in the photograph) recommends brushing the pastry with egg white to prevent it going soggy.

Serves 4
250 g/9 oz shortcrust (basic pie) pastry
600 g/1¼ lb sliced onions
1 tbsp lard or oil
salt, pepper, nutmeg
1 tbsp flour
250 ml/9 fl oz/1 cup milk
250 ml/9 fl oz/1 cup cream
3 eggs
1 egg white
optional: 75 g/3 oz smoked streaky (fatty)
bacon, diced small

Roll out the pastry thinly to fit a 30-cm/12-inch quiche tin and chill. Stew the onions very gently in the lard or oil until pale golden. Season with salt, plenty of black pepper and a good scraping of nutmeg. Stir in the flour and cook for a further 5 minutes.

Whisk together the milk, cream, eggs and salt and pepper to taste. Paint the pastry with egg white, stir the onions into the custard and tip it into the pastry-lined tin. Scatter the bacon cubes on top (if using). Heat the oven to 220°C/425°F/Gas Mark 7 and bake for about 40 minutes or until golden brown. Serve piping hot with green salad and a bottle of Sylvaner or Pinot Blanc to accompany.

LES NOUILLES A L'ALSACIENNE

Pasta seems to have reached Alsace from Italy after the Thirty Years War, and recipes figure in the Abbot Buchinger's 1671 cookbook. Noodles here have a softer texture than in Italy because – explains master (or mistress?) miller Madame Censi of the Moulin Jenny in Hésingue – locally grown soft wheat flour is preferred for making them.

Serves 4
300 g/10 oz/2 cups plain (all-purpose)
white flour
salt
3 eggs
a little oil
butter

Mix together the flour and salt. Add the eggs and droplets of oil or sprinkles of flour as necessary to give a smooth, firm dough which does not stick to your hands (can be done in the food processor). Knead well and leave to rest for at least 1 hour. Dust a large board or table with flour and roll out the dough as thinly as possible to a large rectangle. Dust with flour and roll up like a giant Swiss roll (jelly roll). Cut in fine slices all along its length, then shake out the noodles and dust with flour.

Cook in plenty of boiling salted water with a little oil for about 3 minutes or until just *al dente*. Taste a strand to see if it is done. Drain, return to the pan and toss briefly with some butter, salt and pepper. Serve at once.

Tarte à l'oignon

Coq au Riesling with home-made noodles

COQ AU RIESLING

Simple but delicious, Alsace's answer to coq au vin made with white instead of red wine. Serve with home-made noodles and an excellent Riesling.

Serves 4

1 large chicken or cockerel cleaned and cut in
8 pieces
50 g/2 oz/4 tbsp butter + 1 tbsp oil
4 shallots, finely chopped
300 ml/½ pint/ a generous cup dry white wine
300 ml/½ pint/a generous cup chicken stock
250 g/9 oz mushrooms, quartered
salt and pepper
juice of ½ lemon
6 tbsp double (heavy) cream or *crème fraîche*
plenty of chopped parsley

Dry the pieces of chicken or cockerel well and toss them in a large pan in half the butter and the oil until golden, about 5 minutes on each side. Set aside and in the same fat soften the shallots without browning. Moisten with the wine and the chicken stock; replace the meat. Simmer very gently for 35-40 minutes for chicken (1-1¼ hours for cockerel) or until no pink juices appear when you prick the legs with a skewer near the joint.

Sweat the mushrooms in remaining butter with salt, pepper and lemon juice for 5 minutes. Remove meat from pan and keep warm with the mushrooms. Boil down cooking juices until reduced to about a cupful, then whisk in the cream. Boil again, check the seasoning. Pour on to the meat and mushrooms, sprinkle with parsley.

Variation: for *coq à la bière* (delicious and original), substitute lager for wine.

SOUPE AUX FRUITS ROUGES

Red fruit and black grapes are bathed in a fruit coulis and served chilled. A recipe from chef Pierre Irrmann, whose Restaurant Chambard in Kaysersberg overlooks some of Madame Faller's vines.

Serves 8
Coulis
100 g/4 oz each strawberries, raspberries
and redcurrants
sugar to taste
2 tbsp kirsch

about 1.2 kg/2½ lb assorted fruit
(black grapes, cherries, raspberries,
redcurrants, blackberries etc.)

Clean the fruit for the coulis and purée it in the liquidizer with sugar to taste and kirsch. Prepare the rest of the fruits, put them in a beautiful bowl, toss gently with the fruit coulis and serve well chilled with mint sprigs and vanilla ice cream if wished.

LES GRANDES MAISONS D'ALSACE

*'Un petit verre du vin d'Alsace, c'est comme une robe
légère, une fleur de printemps, c'est le rayon de soleil
qui vient égayer la vie.'*

It is a continual conundrum to wine merchants, writers
and the growers themselves that the fine wines of
Alsace are not better known or more widely appreciated.
In an attempt to tackle this problem, a number of well-
known family firms (Hugel, Trimbach, Beyer, Kuentz-
Bas, Lorentz, Dopff & Irion, Dopff au Moulin and
Schlumberger) have grouped themselves together on the
British market in a loose association known as les Grandes
Maisons d'Alsace. Their objective is to project an image
of the quality wines of Alsace in a market increasingly
challenged by the area's co-operative movement (see
previous chapter on Turckheim, page 126).

Image promotion is their common aim, but the styles
of wine-making of each house (as will be seen from the
following thumbnail sketches) show marked differences
one from another. These differences reflect not only the
conditions peculiar to each vineyard (soils, microcli-
mates, exposure) but also the way each house chooses to
vinify its wines. It is tempting (though not always
accurate) to suppose that people make wine in their own
image . . .

All the Grandes Maisons use each of the seven Alsace
grape varieties, but not all make *crémant* (sparkling
wine). Though their established reputation – which is
considerable, and arguably the cornerstone of the

Nobly rotting Gewurztraminer grapes for a noble wine.
Previous page: *The Ste. Hume chapel and Trimbach vineyard*

reputation of Alsace fine wines throughout the world – has been made with the 'noble grapes' (Riesling, Gewurztraminer, Pinot Gris and Muscat), their wines from 'lesser' varieties (Pinots Blanc and Noir and Sylvaner) provide some delightful drinking – rather on the principle that even a poached egg would be perfect at a three-star restaurant.

Above all, bear in mind that while many growers can make decent wine in a great year, the real test comes in the lesser ones; this is when the great houses come into their own (recent outstanding vintages include '76, '83, '85 and '89).

Opinions among members on the merits (or other-wise) of the recent *grand cru* legislation vary from hostility to enthusiasm, with a heavy dose of indifference in the middle. On the value of the *sigilles*, however (seals awarded by the *Confrérie de St Etienne*, Alsace's equivalent of Burgundy's *Confrérie des Chevaliers du Tastevin*), there is unanimous agreement. Wines submitted for tasting must have a certain bottle age and are thus better able to be judged on their merits than at many press tastings, where wines are often too young to show well; the panel is also, crucially, composed of fellow growers. As Christian Bas of Kuentz-Bas puts it: 'we are judged by our peers'.

In a class of their own are the priceless late harvest (*vendange tardive*) and selected berry (*sélection de grains nobles*) wines, notable and wondrous exceptions to the rule that wines in Alsace are vinified dry. The grapes, some of them affected by noble rot, are picked in November and December (sometimes even as late as January), have very high alcohol and natural sugar levels and result in intensely aromatic wines of varying sweetness and incredible complexity. Their price reflects the risky nature of the enterprise and the tiny quantities involved. The late Jean Hugel (who pioneered the making of such wines in Alsace) observed that they should be enjoyed 'on their own, outside the context of a meal, with your best wine-loving friends, in a respectful atmosphere and without the slightest reference to their price' – which says it all.

LEON BEYER
68420 Eguisheim

In a part of the world where people tend to be short of stature, the Beyer family stand – literally – head and shoulders above the rest. Father Léon, tall, patrician, an eminent *gastronome* and wine connoisseur, decided many years ago to target his wines at top restaurants: Beyer wines feature on the lists of all the three-star Michelin establishments in Europe. This emphasis has shaped the style of their wines: believing that the drier the wine, the better the match with food, they take care to ferment out every last gram of residual sugar. As Marc Beyer observes: 'sugar in wine is like make-up on a woman's face: it masks the imperfections'.

Right: *Riquewihr rooftops and vines*

Endorsing the traditional family links with *la grande restauration*, he recently took a group of top Alsace chefs (Haeberlin, Jung, Husser *et al*) to the east coast of the United States for the centenary celebrations of one of Alsace's more famous exports: the Statue of Liberty. It was a resounding promotional success, both for Alsace's fine wines and for her cuisine, as each chef took over the kitchens of a well-known restaurant or hotel for a week.

Best-known labels include Riesling les Ecaillers and Gewurztraminer les Comtes d'Eguisheim. Discerning commentators admire Beyer wines for their superb firmness, dryness and great ageing potential. They afford an element of challenge to the lover of fine, elegant, characterful wines.

DOPFF & IRION
68340 Riquewihr

Guy Dopff, the delightful, diminutive head of the family business admits with a twinkle that he likes to *drink* wine, not just to *taste* it. It may not be a coincidence, therefore, that his wines are very natural, dry, light and more-ish. He has an engaging way of characterizing the different Alsace grape varieties – Gewurztraminer, for instance, becomes *'le petit Jésus en culotte de velours'*, the little Christ child in velvet trousers.

He is a past President of the Grandes Maisons and five times President of Alsace's official wine body (CIVA). On the recent *grand cru* legislation, he is not alone among GM members in wondering whether what was undoubtedly a good idea in principle (to raise the image of the best wines of Alsace and to encourage excellence) is in the process of going awry. He regrets the increasingly prolific use of vineyard names which confuse the consumer and sound German; he questions the objectivity used in designating the vineyards for *grand cru* status and doubts if quality controls are sufficiently rigorous.

Their best-known (and arguably their finest) wine is Gewurztraminer Les Sorcières – from the Witches' Vineyard. Look out also for their Riesling Les Murailles and Pinot Gris Les Maquisards, the vineyard so-named by his father in honour of the partisans during the war.

DOPFF AU MOULIN
68340 Riquewihr

'Alsace', observes pipe-smoking Pierre-Etienne Dopff somewhat wearily, 'is on the dry side of the Rhine,' referring to the province's perennial problem of distinguishing the style of its wines from that of neighbouring Germany. Though reluctant to comment on the style of Dopff au Moulin wines he is prepared to concede that they probably come closer in style to Trimbach than to Hugel wines – which I interpret to mean very dry wines of great structure and ageing potential.

Since grandfather Julien Dopff pioneered *méthode champenoise* wines in Alsace at the turn of the century, Dopff au Moulin's champagne-method sparkling wines have represented an increasingly important part of the firm's business (nowadays they make up about a quarter

A familiar sight in Alsace

The Hugel sign, by Hansi

of all their wines) and are generally considered to be among the area's finest. They are made mainly from Pinot Blanc, though some Chardonnay is now also being used; the *blanc de noirs* and *rosé* were created to meet consumer demand for pink sparkling wines.

Their seventy hectares (175 acres) of vines include some in the Schoenenburg, Sporen and Brand *grands cru vineyards*; their Eichberg Gewurztraminer is consistently praised. Monsieur Dopff himself describes his '83 late harvest Riesling as 'the best wine in the house'. He expresses disapproval of wood for Alsace's red wine, preferring to make Pinot Noir in the traditional (i.e. light, fruity) style, 'as befits a white wine region'.

HUGEL
68340 Riquewihr

'A family business is like a dairy cow', Jean ('Johnnie') Hugel is fond of saying: 'if everyone milks her, she dries up. If everyone gives her a bit of care and attention, she thrives.' Since 1639, the family cow has been steadily thriving as twelve successive generations have tended to her needs.

Between them the Hugels have also presented a united family front in the battle for the recognition of Alsace wines – particularly the battle on foreign soil. 'Johnnie' Hugel (the English nickname is no coincidence) has made the Anglo-Saxon market his own, and it is largely thanks to his untiring efforts that Hugel wines – and the wines of Alsace in general – are as well known as they are today in the English-speaking world.

Monsieur Hugel has voiced some of the fiercest doubts about the direction in which the much-disputed *grand cru* legislation seems to be leading. While in favour of the *concept* (he points out that he was the first president of the INAO Commission for Alsace *grands crus*), he is completely opposed to the generalized use of vineyard names on labels, names which are inevitably – given Alsace's history – Germanic-sounding and therefore all too easily mistaken for the very product with which they try hard to avoid confusion: German wines.

The family pride themselves on being pioneers. In 1934 they made the region's first *vendange tardive* (late harvest) and *sélection de grains nobles* (selected berry) wines, and in 1983 young Etienne Hugel began maturing some Pinot Noir in small oak barrels bought from Mouton-Rothschild. The resulting full-bodied, mouth-filling red wines, though not universally admired, are good enough to be automatically recommended by the *Meilleur Sommelier du Monde*, Serge Dubs of the Auberge de l'Ill, to any diner requesting a 'proper' red wine from the area (i.e. not a rosé). Hugel wines are massive, rich, beautifully structured, combining the enviable attributes of instant appeal with great longevity.

KUENTZ-BAS
68420 Husseren-les-Châteaux

Kuentz-Bas embody the axiom that small is beautiful. Smallest – but by no means least – of the Grandes Maisons, with only twelve hectares (36 acres) of vineyards, their aim is to have each of their wines express to its fullest potential the grape variety from

which it was made and the *terroir* on which it was grown. The result is tantalizingly tiny lots (*cuvées*), separately vinified and sometimes too small even to feature on their price list, therefore rationed out parsimoniously to the area's top restaurants – often the best source of Kuentz-Bas wines.

Christian Bas has made a particular study of wine with food and the firm annually awards a trophy to a young, enterprising chef who proposes and prepares a dish designed to go with one of their wines. His own favourite marriage is a Muscat d'Alsace (Kuentz-Bas are especially proud of theirs) with asparagus – also from Alsace, of course.

In 1981 the birth of Christian's daughter Caroline coincided with the first late harvest wines produced on the property. Both happy events were immortalized in the Cuvée Caroline label which all subsequent *vendange tardive* wines bear. 1983, the year in which they made their first *sélection de grains nobles* saw the birth of Jérémy, whose name has now joined his sister's in the ranks of Kuentz-Bas' most treasured wines.

LORENTZ
68750 Bergheim

Lorentz wines seem to combine the best of all possible worlds: immediate appeal (thanks to the plumpness – *moelleux* – conferred by a little residual sugar), coupled with great ageing potential (due to the clay-limestone soils on which they are grown). As if to underline this point, Monsieur Lorentz slipped into a superb tasting of the full range of their wines a golden, leggy, powerful wine with an elusive minty aroma. It turned out to be a '59 Muscat d'Alsace. The classic Muscat grapiness had gone, leaving a wine whose balance and structure belied its thirty years.

Left: *Vineyards near Husseren-les-Chateaux*

The house of Lorentz

Under the names of Jérome and Gustave Lorentz, the firm owns thirty hectares (75 acres) of vines in and around the village of Bergheim, of which half fall in *grand cru* vineyards. The bulk are in the Altenberg vineyard where Riesling, Pinot Gris and Gewurztraminer are all grown; a few are in the Kanzlerberg vineyard. 'Rich', 'fat', 'powerful' are adjectives frequently used to describe Lorentz wines. Their Gewurztraminer Altenberg is superb, luscious yet not overblown. Good vintages (some of the more recent ones still available include '83 and '85) should be squirrelled away and left to mature for at least ten years; the problem, as always with Lorentz wines, is that they are irresistible now.

DOMAINES SCHLUMBERGER
68500 Guebwiller

It is difficult to conceive of any reason for going to Guebwiller other than to sample some of the Domaine Schlumberger's smiling wines. So benevolent is the climate of this otherwise unsmiling town that the firm's biggest problem in good years is to hold down the alcohol levels and allow the delicate nuances in their wines to emerge: a constant battle, in fact, between concentration and finesse.

Today's huge 140-hectare (350-acre) vineyard dominating Guebwiller grew from a mere twenty hectares (fifty acres) which previously belonged to the nearby Abbey of Murbach and were bought in 1810 by the industrialist Nicholas Schlumberger. After the successive horrors of phylloxera and the First World War, the vineyards were sold and the land reverted to scrub. Today, patient buying back and rebuilding by the family has resulted in the biggest single *domaine* under one owner. With four *grands crus* (Kitterlé, Kessler, Spiegel

and Saering) under their belt, Schlumberger are very much in favour of the new legislation. Eveline Beydon-Schlumberger is emphatic, however, about the benefits for Alsace as a whole: good for the image, good for standards, above all good because by adopting the very French concept of *grands crus*, Alsace has been put fairly and squarely into the French wine-growing camp.

For a real treat to partner a Christmas *foie gras*, seek out a Schlumberger Cuvée Christine late harvest Gewurztraminer. For outstanding everyday drinking, their deep-golden, honeyed Pinot Blanc is hard to beat.

F. E. TRIMBACH
68150 Ribeauvillé

Trimbach wines are grown-up stuff, not for the young and impatient. They need time to develop in the bottle, time also for leisured, lingering enjoyment from the glass. In order to ensure that at least the first point is respected, the firm only releases wines onto the market when they are considered ready for drinking, which may be anything between three and seven years after bottling, depending on grape variety and vintage.

'Austerity' is a word which crops up frequently in connection which Trimbach wines, an epithet which had always bothered me with its overtones of harshness and inaccessibility. The clay-limestone soils which predominate in the family's sixty to seventy hectares (150 acres) of vines, coupled with Bernard Trimbach's chosen style of vinification (rigid temperature control, very early bottling, scrupulous avoidance of malolactic fermentation) certainly combine to produce wines which are slow to mature and very closed up when young. However, after a morning's tasting with Jean Trimbach, a notably un-austere member of this great family, 'austerity' was unanimously outvoted in favour of 'restrained elegance'.

Harvesting at Niedermorschwihr

En route to Ribeauvillé

Trimbach wines are widely encountered throughout France in places where it matters: at the Elysée Palace, for instance, or *chez* Bocuse at his sixtieth birthday party. Exports account for about two-thirds of sales; in the US some twenty-six per cent of all Alsace wines are Trimbach's. Ribeauvillé is Riesling-land, and the firm are probably best known for their Cuvée Frédéric Emile and the priceless Clos Ste Hune (sometimes referred to – though never by them – as the Romanée Conti of Alsace). Restrained elegance is also a feature of their Gewurztraminer Cuvée des Seigneurs de Ribeaupierre. Their Pinot Blanc, chosen by the Haeberlin family on the occasion of chef Paul's decoration with the *Légion d'Honneur*, is a delight.

FROM RASPBERRIES TO HOLLY BERRIES

Given a glimmer of a chance, the *alsacien* will distil practically anything he can lay his hands on. The fact is, though, that his opportunity to do so has been severely curtailed since 1953 when a law was passed decreeing a steep tax on home distilling, except in those families where the *droit local* (hereditary distilling right) already existed. Some mourn its passing, notably Alsace's Député Grussenmeyer who has made himself famous by campaigning tirelessly in the Chambre des Députés to have the law revoked; others remember ruefully the bad old days when the average family consumption of *eau de vie* was between thirty and fifty litres per year, and the countryman or -woman's breakfast consisted of a couple of milk rolls dunked in a glass of '*schnapps*', the generic name in Alsace for *eau de vie* of any flavour.

The origins of fruit distilling in Alsace are much disputed: it is not clear whether the *Kirsewin* and *Kirsenwasser* mentioned in fifteenth- and sixteenth-century texts were actually distilled from cherries, or were simply a grape brandy in which the fruit had been macerated. Whatever the process, it is generally agreed that the purpose was originally medicinal – as indeed the name (meaning 'water of life') suggests. In 1650 a monk with alchemist inclinations evidently had the bright idea of boiling up fermented cherries in the hope of finding a cure for cholera. Uses other than the purely medicinal were gradually perceived, though the digestive prop-erties of *eaux de vie* are still invoked by many.

Alsace shares its distilling tradition with Switzerland,

the Black Forest and Lorraine – though some of the fruits and berries used in Alsace tend to raise a few eyebrows with the neighbours. The market is divided locally between the big names like Wolfberger (owned by the giant Eguisheim co-operative); the smaller, private firms such as Monsieur de Miscault's in Lapoutroie (owner of the delightful Musée des Eaux de Vie); and finally the *bouilleurs de cru* or 'boilers of raw spirit'.

Though this wonderful title evokes images of illicit stills, surreptitious boilings of sinister plants and midnight raids by the local police, some families, as already mentioned, still enjoy the right to distil – untaxed – a small amount of spirit for domestic consumption. Thus, provided they do not make more than their entitlement, nor commercialize any part of their production, what they brew up is entirely legal (sometimes even drinkable). Some own their own stills, others rent the equipment for a day or two. A familiar sight is a battered old copper still trundling around the countryside on the back of a van, doubtless destined for someone's cellar to mop up the year's excess cherry crop. In the valley of Lapoutroie alone, there are reputed to be eighty stills, of which about half are known to be functioning. On a recent visit to the area, however, we found two of them (presumably the property of some over-zealous *bouilleur de cru*) sitting disconsolately in Monsieur de Miscault's yard, crippled by the Customs and Excise man and donated to the museum, which suggests that their number may now have dwindled somewhat.

The cognac or malt whisky distilling process is the one most commonly used in Alsace. The fruit is fermented and then either distilled immediately, or sealed in a container until needed. There follow two distillations to arrive at the finished *eau de vie*; the first produces a relatively light alcohol, while from the

Monsieur Latscha brewing up the mash

Copper still in the Musée des Eaux de Vie, *Lapoutroie*

second boiling comes the full-strength *eau de vie*. Only the 'heart' of the matter (the spirit produced at the middle of the process), is retained, and it is in selecting *le coeur* that all the skill of the distiller comes into play. The 'heads' and 'tails' (the unpalatable and powerful spirit produced at the beginning and end) are drawn off and put back in the pot with a fresh lot of fermented fruit, to begin the process once more. Berries and plants which lack the necessary sugar to ferment under their own steam are macerated in a grape brandy and distilled only once.

The Wolfberger distillery, on the other hand, prefer to use a combination of the cognac and armagnac processes. As director Monsieur Camus explains, the latter process (which is shorter) is better suited to delicate fruits, and preserves to the full all their fragile aromas. Their prize-winning pear Williamine is thus a blend of *eaux de vie* from the two different methods.

Some fruit brandies (notably kirsch) benefit from ageing, which mellows the flavour and softens the alcoholic blow. Monsieur de Miscault's eyes light up at the recollection of an 1881 kirsch residing patiently in his attic. Traditionally, ageing was carried out in *bonbonnes* (demijohns) encased in wickerwork and stored under the roof where the dramatic fluctuations in temperature were said to add complexity and flavour to the finished brandy. The modern way, in stainless steel or glass vats, though somehow lacking the romance of the attic, is clearly more practical.

Fruit brandies play an important part in the gastronomy of Alsace – no killing of the fatted calf is complete without a little *digestif*, and many a Sunday afternoon meeting with the builder or architect has been smoothed by the passing of *un petit verre* (a little glass). Nevertheless in comparison with other spirits, they are a drop in

A collection of fruit brandies in the Musée des Eaux de vie

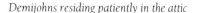

Demijohns residing patiently in the attic

the ocean – albeit a particularly prized drop. Best known are kirsch, *poire* Williams, mirabelle, *quetsch* plum, raspberry and *marc de Gewurztraminer*. *Marc* is also made from Muscat, Pinot Gris and Pinot Noir. Rarest of all are the spirits distilled from wild berries and plants; holly, wild service, sloes, rowan, rosehip (inelegantly known as *gratte-cul*), blackberry, bilberry, elderberry, gentian, juniper, pine and cumin seed.

To enjoy them to the full, some suggest chilling (but not freezing) *eaux de vie* and serving them in large brandy balloon glasses which allow room for the aromas and flavours to unfold subtly on the nose and palate. Others swear by the more traditional way: a shot in the emptied (and still warm) coffee cup, which gives a rougher, more potent effect.

A powerful sedative for fractious children at lengthy *alsacien* feasts is a sugar lump ducked into a glass of spirit: *un canard*. The final option is not to drink *eaux de vie* at all, but simply to take a good sniff: the aroma (particularly of raspberry and of pear) is so exquisitely true that the taste is almost an anti-climax.

TERRINE DE LAPIN AUX MIRABELLES

A basic recipe for a rabbit terrine with mirabelle plums and brandy. For a change try using other meats, fruit or eau de vie.

Serves 8-10
a 1½ kg/3 lb rabbit, skinned and
gutted (keep liver)
300 g/10 oz lean, boneless pork
300 g/10 oz pork back fat
2 tsp salt
freshly ground black pepper
4 tbsp *eau de vie de mirabelle*
carrot, onion, bouquet garni
a little oil
1 egg
200 g/7 oz mirabelle plums, stoned
(pitted) and chopped
2 sprigs of thyme

Strip all the meat from the rabbit; reserve some strips for the garnish. Chop the rest roughly with the pork and fat. Put in a bowl with salt and pepper and half the *eau de vie*. Marinate for at least 6 hours, or overnight.

Chop up the bones and make a rich rabbit stock with the carrot, onion, bouquet garni and water to cover. Simmer for 2 hours; strain and reduce to about half a cup of syrupy liquid.

Season the reserved rabbit strips and stiffen them in a little very hot oil with the liver (if available). Sprinkle with the remaining *eau de vie* and leave to cool. Chop the marinated rabbit meat, pork and fat very finely in the food processor. Add the stock and the egg. Beat well to lighten the mixture. Stir in the chopped liver and mirabelle plums.

Lay one sprig of thyme in the bottom of a 1.4 kg/3 lb terrine, pack in half the mixture, press the reserved rabbit strips into it, and finish with the rest of the mixture and the remaining thyme. Cover with foil and a lid and bake in a bain-marie at 180°C/350°F/ Gas Mark 4 for 1¼ to 1½ hours. The terrine is done when it feels firm and springy; a skewer inserted into the middle will feel uncomfortably hot to the cheek. Cool, chill. Keep 4-5 days before eating.

CREPES FARCIES A L'ALSACIENNE

Crêpes with fromage blanc and fruit filling. A recipe from Monsieur Kiener, Auberge du Schoenenbourg, Riquewihr.

Crêpes (about 24)
125 g/4½ oz/scant cup plain (all purpose) white flour
3 tbsp sugar
pinch of salt
4 tbsp melted butter
3 eggs
350 ml/generous pint/1½ cups milk (or milk/water)
1 tsp vanilla essence (extract)
2 tbsp kirsch
Filling (per person)
2 tbsp curd (farmer's or pot) cheese (*fromage blanc*)
2 tbsp double (heavy) cream
sugar to taste
2 strawberries
6 raspberries or 3 tbsp wild strawberries

Blend together the crêpe ingredients and make up thin, lacy crêpes 15 cm/6 inches diameter (allow 2-3 per person). Whisk together the curd cheese, cream and sugar. Fold in the fruit. Stuff crêpes and fold over. Put in a buttered and sugared ovenproof dish and chill until needed.

Heat the oven to 230°C/450°F/Gas Mark 8 and bake for a few minutes until the filling is tepid and the crêpes lightly golden. Sprinkle with icing (confectioners') sugar and serve with a fruit coulis.

SOUFFLE GLACE AU MARC DE GEWURZTRAMINER DE MARIE-CLAUDE

A delectable way to savour the aromas of marc de gewurz; freeze it in a kugelhopf mould and it becomes kugelhopf glacé.

Makes about 2 litres/4 pints/2 quarts serving 8-10
6 egg yolks
½ glass Gewurztraminer
200 g/7 oz/1 cup sugar
6 tbsp *marc de Gewurztraminer*
½ litre/1 pint/2 cups double (heavy) cream
3 egg whites

Beat together the yolks, Gewurztraminer and half the sugar in a bowl over near-simmering water until very light and fluffy. Cool. Stir in the *marc*. Beat the cream to soft peaks. Whisk the egg whites till stiff but not dry, then add the remaining sugar and continue beating to a meringue-like consistency. Fold all three preparations together and freeze, either in individual cups or as ice cream. Serve with a salad of halved, pipped grapes, or a fruit coulis.

(For 1 litre/2 pints/1 quart *soufflé glacé*, use 3 yolks, 2 tbsp wine or water, 100 g/4 oz/½ cup sugar, 4 tbsp *marc de gewurz*, 250 ml/9 fl oz/1 cup cream and 2 whites.)

Soufflé glacé au marc de Gewurztraminer

Select bibliography

Bock, Jérome, *Kraüterbuch*, 1551 edition

Buchinger, *Kochbuch*, 1671

Curnonsky, *Guide des merveilles culinaires et des bonnes auberges françaises – L'Alsace*, 1921

Comité Interprofessionel du Vin d'Alsace, *Le guide des grands crus d'Alsace*

Delpal, Jacques-Louis, *Alsace*, Fernand Nathan 1981

Doerflinger, Marguerite, & Klein, Georges, *Toute la gastronomie alsacienne (plats salés et plats sucrés)*, Mars & Mercure, 1978 & 1979

Drischel, Poulain & Truchelut, *Histoire et recettes de l'Alsace gourmande*, Privat, 1988

Egen, Jean, *Les tilleuls de Lautenbach*, 1986

Eloges (various), Saisons d'Alsace no. 20, 1966

Erckmann-Chatrian, *L'Ami Fritz*, Livres de poche

Gaertner, Pierre, & Frédérick, Robert, *La cuisine alsacienne*, Flammarion, 1979

Gérard, Charles, *L'ancienne Alsace à table*, 1862

Haeberlin, Paul & Jean-Pierre, *Les recettes de l'Auberge de l'Ill*, Flammarion, 1982

Johnson, Hugh, *The Wine Companion*, Mitchell Beazley, 1983

Kohler, Irène, *La cuisine alsacienne* Lorraine-Alsace Diffusion, 1974

Lallemand, Roger, *La vraie cuisine de l'Alsace,* Editions Quartiers Latin

Layton, T. A., *Wines and People of Alsace,* Cassell, 1970

Michelin Green Guide: Vosges, 3rd edition

Parker, Robert, *The Wine Buyer's Guide*, Dorling Kindersley, 1988

Pudlowski, Gilles, *La jeune cuisine alsacienne*, Albin Michel 1986

Renvoisé, Guy, *Guide des Vins d'Alsace*, Solarama, 1983

Schneider, Tony & Jean-Louis, & Brison, Danièle, *La cuisine alsacienne*, Bueb & Reumaux, 1985

Spoerlin, Marguerite, née Baumgartner *Oberrheinisches Kochbuch*, Risler Mulhouse, 1829 & 1833; French edition *La cuisinière du Haut-Rhin*, 1842

Streicher, Fischer & Blèze, *Histoire des alsaciens*, Fernand Nathan, 1979

Vandyke Price, Pamela, *Alsace Wines*, Sotheby Publications, 1984

Voegeling, François, *La gastronomie alsacienne*, Editions des Dernières Nouvelles d'Alsace – ISTRA

Wedgwood, C.V., *The Thirty Years War*, Cape, 1938

Acknowledgements

The many people who helped the pieces of this book fall into place are mentioned in the text. To others who would otherwise remain anonymous, I am no less grateful: Christiane Bisch, ('La cuisinière du Bas-Rhin') provided many valuable introductions and support; Monsieur Pierre Bouard of CIVA gave a helpful overview of the Alsace wine world; Monsieur René Claude of Chavannes-sur-l'Étang enlightened me further on the art of *choucroute* and Monsieur Courroy of Rupt-sur-Moselle on Munster cheese, while Madame Marchal provided a memorable post-photographic breakfast. Monsieur Bildstein of Saisons d'Alsace patiently photocopied reams of pertinent documents now out of print; Monsieur Georges Klein, former curator of the Musée Alsacien in Strasbourg and Monsieur Niess, director of the Tourism Office in Colmar both provided many introductions. My family – as always – were endlessly supportive and generally wonderful.

INDEX

Note: Numbers in italic denote illustration

Asparagus 22-6, 22-9, 27, 28, 115
Aumonières aux griottes 116, 117

Baeckeoffe 57, 57
Beef 57, 130
Beignets de courgettes 79
Bettelmann 79
Betteraves, salade de 78
Bœuf gros sel à l'alsacienne 130
Bread 12, 31, 35, 36, 37, 77, 86
Bunner, Madame 75, 77

Cassolette d'escargots au Riesling 63
Cheese 28, 85, 86, 93
Cherries 79, 116, 139
Chicken 123, 139
Choucroute 16, 45-7, 48, 48, 49
Co-operatives 126-29
    Bennwihr 126
    Eguisheim 126
    Ingersheim 126
    Kientzheim 126
    Pfaffenheim 126
    Ribeauvillé 126
    Turckheim 129
Coq au Riesling 138, 139
Courgette, fritters 79
Crémant d'Alsace (méthode champenoise) 21,
    119, 140, 144
Crêpes farcies à l'alsacienne 156

Edelzwicker 21, 26, 84, 129
Escalopes de foie gras aux pommes reinettes 43
Escargots en raviole aux graines de pavot 64, 65

Feuilleté aux deux saumons à la choucroute 50
    de pigeonneau au chou et aux truffes 101
Fish and shellfish 102, 114, 130
Flammekueche 95
Foie gras 38-41, 40, 41, 42, 42, 43, 50, 101, 115,
    148
Fondue aux quatre fromages 85
Freund-lich Gewurztraminer cup 85
Fruit 85, 110, 116, 124, 139, 155, 156
Gâteaux de foies blonds de volaille 107, 107
Gateau de gambas au Riwele 121, 121
Gewurztraminer 21, 43, 85, 85, 126, 128, 129,
    130, 142, 142, 144, 145, 147, 149

Ham 58, 59

Jambon en croûte 58, 59

Kidneys 116
Kugelhopf 30, 77
    au lard 36
    surprise 36, 37

Lamb 57, 109
Lapereau, dodine de 120, 120
Lasagne de poussins aux petits légumes 122, 123
Lewerknepfle 94
Liver 94, 107

Matelote protestante d'Illhauesern 102, 103
    de poissons de mer au Gewurztraminer 130, 131
Mousse aux asperges, petites 27
Muscat 21, 34, 119, 128, 129, 135, 142, 147
Mushrooms 102, 115, 123
Munster 20, 68, 69, 82, 82, 85

Nouilles à l'alsacienne 136

Pain paysan de Madame Hell 86, 87
Pains au pavot 35
    au lait, petits 35
Palette de porc 71
Pasta, dough 136
    dishes using 64, 115, 123
Pâté chaud alsacien 56
Pigeon 101
Pinot Blanc 21, 128, 136, 142, 145, 149
Pinot Gris 21, 128, 135, 142, 144, 147
Pinot Noir 21, 90, 128, 135, 142, 145
Pommes de terres coiffées de Munster 86
Pork 48, 49, 52-5, 56, 57, 58
Potatoes 71, 86
Pot-au-feu d'agneau aux poivrons rouges 108, 109
    d'escargots à l'étoile d'anis 63
    de foie gras au gros sel 43

Quiche à la choucroute 49

Rabbit 120, 155
Ravioles de ris de veau aux asperges et aux
    champignons sauvages 115, 115
Restaurants:
    à l'Aigle, Pfulgriesheim 92, 95
    l'Auberge de l'Ill, Illhauesern 98-100
    Aux Armes de France, Ammerschwihr 118-19
    Le Cerf, Marlenheim 111-13
    Chez Yvonne, Strasbourg 88-90
    Le Crocodile, Strasbourg 105-6

Riesling 21, 48, 49, 57, 63, 102, 107, 128, 134,
    135, 139, 142, 144, 145, 147, 148
Rognonnade de veau à l'âche de montagne 116
Roïgabragelti 71

Salade de betteraves 78, 78
    de cervelas et Gruyère 93, 93
    de pissenlits au lard et aux œufs durs 71
    de printemps aux asperges et au Gruyère 28
    de volaille tiède à la choucroute 49
Salads 28, 49, 71, 78, 93
Sausages 52-5, 55
Schieffala 71
Schillinger, chef 40, 41
Sélection de grains nobles 142
Snails 60, 60, 62, 63, 64
Soufflé glacé au marc de Gewurztraminer 156, 157
Soupe aux fruits rouges 139, 139
Spätzle 56
Sweetbreads 115
Sylvaner 21, 62, 129, 135, 136, 142

Tarte à l'oignon 20, 136, 137
    au fromage blanc 102
    aux myrtilles 73, 73
    chaude aux asperges 28, 29
    flambée 90-2, 95, 95
Tartelettes flambées 94
Terrine de lapin aux mirabelles 155
Tourte de la Vallée de Munster 72, 72
    vosgienne 58

Vacherins glacés aux fruits 124, 125
Veal 54, 116
Velouté froid à l'oseille aux quenelles de saumon
    114, 114
Vendanges tardive 142, 145, 148

Wine 10, 11, 12, 13, 16, 17, 18, 20, 84, 88,
    126-29, 134-35, 140-49
Wine growers:
    Leon Beyer 142-43
    Domaines Schlumberger 147-48
    Dopff au Moulin 144-45
    Dopff et Irion 144
    Madame Faller 132-35
    Hugel et fils 142, 145
    Josmeyer 62, 100
    Kuentz-Bas 145-46
    Lorentz 147
    F. E. Trimbach 148-49
    Zind-Humbrecht 100